When the Spirit Descends

To order additional copies of
When the Spirit Descends, by Jan Paulsen,
call 1-800-765-6955.

Visit our website at *www.reviewandherald.com* for
information on other Review and Herald products.

When the Spirit Descends

Jan Paulsen

REVIEW AND HERALD® PUBLISHING ASSOCIATION
HAGERSTOWN, MD 21740

The author assumes full responsibility for the accuracy of all facts and quotations as cited in this book.

All biblical references, except where otherwise indicated, are from *The New English Bible.* © The Delegates of the Oxford University Press and the Syndics of the Cambridge University Press 1970. Reprinted by permission.

Texts credited to NIV are from the *Holy Bible, New International Version.* Copyright © 1973, 1978, 1984, International Bible Society. Used by permission of Zondervan Bible Publishers.

Bible texts credited to RSV are from the Revised Standard Version of the Bible, copyright © 1946, 1952, 1971, by the Division of Christian Education of the National Council of the Churches of Christ in the U.S.A. Used by permission.

This book was
Edited by Richard W. Coffen
Copyedited by Delma Miller and James Cavil
Designed by Bill Kirstein
Electronic makeup by Shirley M. Bolivar
Typeset: 12/13 Bembo

PRINTED IN U.S.A.
05 04 03 02 01 5 4 3 2 1

R&H Cataloging Service
Paulsen, Jan
When the Spirit descends.

1. Holy Spirit. I. Title

231.3

ISBN 0-8280-1448-5

Contents

Preface

During two consecutive years I delivered a series of lectures on the doctrine of the Holy Spirit to theology students at Newbold College. It has also been my privilege to have addressed this same subject in several churches and at gatherings of pastors. I left these occasions amazed (and depressed) by the extent to which loyal, committed Christians saw the Holy Spirit as an enigma and, to a large extent, Someone yet to come.

There is, apparently, a common opinion that the main reason for spiritual failure is that the Spirit's arrival to God's people has been delayed. Consequently, Christians have been led, or have led themselves, to account for their spiritual shortcomings by looking elsewhere than to their own apathy, occasioned by their own worldliness.

Some Christians, concerned by their own spiritual state, and longing for a richer life, permitted themselves—although, of course, not admitting it—an occasional quick peep through tiny cracks in the "ecclesiastical walls" to observe the activities and exercises of so-called "Spirit-filled" Christians of the Pentecostal and charismatic strain. But this only added to their confusion.

My impetus for this study lies in this situation. What I am sharing is the result of my search for clear biblical answers to how the Holy Spirit functions and what His ministry is.

Actually, this book is a reedited, reissued version of the book by the same title, which I wrote some 25 years ago. The publisher has revived it because it feels that the content continues to be relevant to the church. However, the style and language tend to reflect my work from an earlier period.

Introduction

In the early 1930s British writer Samuel Chadwick did something unusual for his day: he wrote a book about the Holy Spirit. Many will doubt his claim that "the last great book on the Spirit was written in 1674."[1] Probably even more will question whether his own book is a "great" one. Nevertheless, Chadwick's point was well taken. The doctrine of the Holy Spirit was not widely studied among Christians. And he saw this as a sign of spiritual death in the church. To some the expectation of death may be frightening. But once death has arrived, it disturbs none of its victims. To be disturbed, one has to be alive.

In many of the historical churches Christianity eventually disintegrated into a set of formal confessional statements, without an experience. The Holy Spirit thus came to be the "neglected person of the Godhead." To an increasing number of Christians who were still alive and alert this was a sign of advanced decay.

The diagnosis may seem plausible. But before we shout an unreserved amen, a word of caution is in order. Has it not always been a feature of the Holy Spirit to call attention not to Himself but to the other Witness (John 14:26; 15:26)? Is it not the Spirit's proclamation of that other Witness, Jesus Christ, that leads many to an understanding of the gospel of salvation, as we see from Paul's experience at Ephesus (Acts 19:4, 5)? And is not that the way the Holy Spirit becomes a force to be reckoned with in the life of every believer? (We shall return to these points later.)

For many years now Pentecostalism has been proclaiming that there is Someone called the Holy Spirit, who, on the whole, is an alien in most Christian churches. Consequently, many Christians have begun to wonder aloud if there might not be an additional dimension to Christianity that they have failed to recognize. These people—and the number steadily increases—come from all walks of life and all churches, covering the whole spectrum from the Methodist, Lutheran, and Reformed churches to the Anglican/Episcopalian, and Roman Catholic constituencies. They do not wish to abandon their churches for other forms of fellowship. But on hearing loud hallelujahs and shouts of victory from the Pentecostal camp, and by stretching to look over the religious fence into a community hitherto considered far too enthusiastic, many of them have begun to feel a sense of spiritual deprivation.

Voices, mostly young voices, can now be heard saying that Christianity in the historical churches has become lethargic and mediocre. "The mainline churches have lost their spiritual vitality!" "The power of Pentecost must be rediscovered!" "Sure it was great to experience conversion, but that was five years ago and has gone stale on me! Am I not entitled to a 'second honeymoon'?" Against this background a quest for charismatic renewal has begun in many churches.

As many set out to experience what is often labeled "baptism in the Holy Spirit," they find guidance reading about the Spirit-happenings recorded in the book of Acts, supplemented by Paul's list of supernatural graces in 1 Corinthians 12:8-11. These earnest readers find an accent on healing, prophesying, and, especially, speaking in tongues, at times innocently spoken of as just "praying together." It holds an attraction because it offers a departure from the staid confessional statements of traditional Christianity to a "spontaneous and dynamic experience of religion" in which personal victory is achieved *now.* At least that is what the adherents of the charismatic movement claim. For them the long, sluggish grind of the Christian walk may be abbreviated to the instantaneous experience of Spirit baptism. It is held that only those who become thus involved can truly confess belief in the Holy Spirit. At this point in history, people who subscribe to this concept constitute no small fragment of Christendom.

Against (literally *against*) this camp is an even larger community of committed Christians from many churches (to say nothing of the deadweight and impotent Christians) who are frightened and confused by, or downright hostile toward, this kind of revivalism. Some are fearful because they feel insecure and uncertain about their own Christian experience and about what God is saying to them. Some are confused because, if this is the Spirit, He is, they think, saying many strange things and operating in many unfamiliar ways. In addition, other loud voices abound, making it difficult to hear His voice in this spiritual jungle. Furthermore, these Christians are hostile because they genuinely believe that the Spirit is not there. The so-called renewal exercises strike them as either self-induced, the product of various pressures, or simply the backyard where the devil is taking his exercise. To them the whole situation is one flourishing on, and please excuse this strong language, "impoverished soil and dunghills."[2]

And yet, however unsympathetic our assessment of these happenings may be, we cannot dismiss them outright. The very fact that charismatic renewal exercises are there in legion must surely say something to the church. And if the church cannot detect that, the chances are that its hearing is very bad.

The duty of every pastor, teacher of religion, and youth counselor is neither to shout "unclean" nor to head for the "ravine of Kerith"—as Elijah did (1 Kings 17:3)—at the first sight of these phenomena. Rather they must "bring them all to the test and then keep what is good" without violating the Spirit (1 Thess. 5:21). Having done *that,* it may be that the proclamation "unclean" will be justified. That must, however, come not as a response to ignorance, fear, and spiritual disarray, but as a clear response to the Spirit's refusal to identify Himself with these renewal happenings.

Of course, one asks immediately: How does the Spirit communicate? How is one to know not only what He says but how He acts? The study that follows in this book will seek answers to these questions.

This book is not intended to be an exhaustive study of the *doctrine* of the Holy Spirit. Instead, it will look at what the Bible says about the Spirit, His role, and His ways of acting. Only when set against a background of biblical orientation is it safe to assess features of current charismatic phenomena.

Three points should be kept in mind.

1. One must exercise care not to read current charismatic phenomena back into the Bible record. There is a danger of assuming an identity that is yet to be established. In other words, charismatic manifestations in the early church, whether in Jerusalem or Corinth, are not necessarily identical with the so-called charismatic renewal movements of today.

2. Some argue that what happened to the first Christians is a pattern for what must continue to happen—that spiritual phenomena are repetitive simply because they happened to the first believers. I do not believe that this is necessarily so. But there is a real sense in which history is *not* repeatable. A lot of water has run under the bridge since apostolic times. It is impossible to reerect in our lives the original setting in history and culture of the early church. There were needs then that are no longer with us simply because their situation 2,000 years ago differs from ours today.

3. Charismatic phenomena are in a way neutral in color. An event that strikes me as supernatural says noth-

ing about where it comes from, or, for that matter, what it *really* is. The actuality of an event makes neither its origin nor its true nature clear. It must be examined, and in doing so we must remember that the genuine and counterfeit sometimes need close, prayerful examination to be told apart. "When the Lord has a genuine channel of light, there are always plenty of counterfeits."[3]

Criteria for identification lie *outside* the phenomenon itself, and these criteria must be of such a character that the *mind* can come to grips with them. Sensory perception provides very fertile soil for gullibility. The faculties of seeing and hearing cannot always be trusted in this delicate task.

Finally, permit me to share a few reflections on the concept that the Spirit is one of the Trinity.

The church of the third and fourth centuries, faced with heretics and schismatics, paused at various intersections to encapsulate its doctrines into creedal statements. One of the formulas to emerge during that time was: "Trinity in unity" = trinity of persons = unity of essence. That may sound vague. Most of us find the formula (and probably any definition of the Trinity) difficult to grasp in the main because there is really nothing in the phenomena of nature to serve as an analogy to it. The analogy, used by some of the mystics, of the human being as spirit, soul, and body, is clearly of no help. Not only is it highly doubtful that a human being can actually be divided in this fashion, but even if it were possible we would still be talking about just *one* person.

Some theologians have actually ended up with a definition of the Trinity as three different modes of existence of one and the same Being. In other words, He is just one. At one point in time (namely, the Old Testament) He was seen as God the Father. Then He turned a few degrees and could be recognized as the Son, Jesus Christ. Finally, after turning a few more degrees (namely, after the

Ascension and Pentecost), the side of Him that we now see came to be known as the Holy Spirit. In all, however, He is just *one* being.

But such an explanation seems hardly acceptable. We need only point to the fact that Jesus Christ looked upon the Father, from whom He had come and to whom He prayed, as well as the *"another* Comforter," as beings entirely other than Himself (John 14:17).

The hard and often impermeable division that the Occidental mind makes between persons (or personalities) adds to our problem of grasping the Trinity. It differs from Jewish thinking, in which individuals, though separate, could still be thought of as blending together or flowing into each other. The Jewish mind (and we must not forget that our biblical statements about God are, on the whole, crops grown in Jewish soil) is likely to have had less of a problem with the whole concept of "Trinity in unity" than we have.

The creedal statement referred to above means that though the Three are separate individuals, They are one in substance, plan, and purpose. The members of the triune Godhead have a common mission and goal. God the Father, God the Son, and God the Holy Spirit act in complement to One Another in history.

The Holy Spirit is as much a part of this division and unity and commonness in mission as are the other two persons of the Godhead. Just as Jesus is an individual external to those whom He seeks to save, so the Holy Spirit is also external. This is important for us to remember so that we can avoid subjectivizing the Spirit in a way that makes Him identical with our own spiritual experience. The Spirit cannot be assimilated with an individual's personal quality of Spirit-filledness. Although the promise is that God will put His Spirit *within* His people (Eze. 36:26, 27), in a very real sense He is *apart* from every human being in that He comes from outside. He is not intrinsically part of any yearning for self-realization that I might have, and what He complements is not my yearning, but the mission of the Father and the Son. Clearly the Spirit is not an element conjured up in my personal reaching out for renewal.

Therefore, the fact that one has had a "spiritual experience," with or without charismatic manifestations, in which one's longings have found fulfillment, cannot of itself be assumed to be the result of the workings of the Holy Spirit. With what right can we assume that the Holy Spirit will ever aid *our* personal or communal movement toward self-realization—evasive as that term may be? Why may He not be entitled to impede that process or give an entirely new direction to it? Is not the *Paraclete* (the Greek word translated "Comforter" in the King James Version of John's Gospel) as much of a prosecuting attorney as a comforter?

The Holy Spirit is God, but He is also the way in which God expresses Himself during the end-time. The Spirit is an immense force beyond anything we have faculty for measuring. By looking back into the history of God's people, we can see in part how He acted, but His work is not yet done. Surely we must not assume that His originality has been depleted and that He will display no unfamiliarity of action.

We are part of a movement in which the Spirit of God acts. It is not possible for us, as committed Christians, to step aside and look at His actions from a distance. But that may be good, for were we able to do that we could not be part of that which the Spirit offers. Finding the balance between knowing the way the Spirit has led, acted, and spoken in the past, and at the same time remaining open to His newness and recognizing that He will not now discredit or invalidate His own past is no easy and straightforward task. But we really have no choice. We must seek this balance in order to be open to the Spirit without being "led down the garden path" by counterfeit spirits.

---

[1] S. Chadwick, *The Way to Pentecost* (London: Hodder and Stoughton, 1972, impr.), p. 9.

[2] *Ibid.*, p. 13.

[3] Ellen G. White, *Selected Messages* (Washington, D.C.: Review and Herald Pub. Assn., 1958), book 2, p. 22.

CHAPTER 1

The Holy Spirit in the Old Testament

To what extent was Israel of old able to think of God in Trinitarian terms? To what extent is it possible for us to formulate concepts of the Trinity based on the Old Testament?

As we read the Old Testament today we may have little difficulty in finding the Son of God present as the preexistent one in Israelite history. We meet Him in prophecies and symbols as the coming Messiah. And, similarly, many will feel fairly clear about the Holy Spirit in the Old Testament (for example, Isa. 63:10, 11; Eze. 37; Joel 2:28, 29).

However, we must keep in mind that we read the Old Testament through the eyes of later revelation, which helps us to make our identifications. Furthermore, God has emerged in history in unique, precise, and unmistakable ways since the Old Testament was given. Centuries elapsed during the interval from the time the last Old Testament book was written to the time when Jesus Christ came into the human family, died, and was resurrected. Jesus provides the clearest revelation of God to date. Whenever I pause to conceive of God, my mind moves spontaneously to the life and mission of Christ. The Christ-event works as a magnet on my mind. My statements about God are shaped by it.

Pentecost was equally a real event in history.

Whenever we speak about Jesus Christ or the Holy Spirit, we do so against a background of what has already happened in history, namely, the cross/resurrection weekend followed by Pentecost. So we may read the Old Testament and appreciate its Trinitarian references simply because we read it from a post-Passover and post-Pentecost position.

Old Testament times were not days when Israel thought of God in Trinitarian terms. Their monotheism, which they guarded jealously—much of the time, at least—against the polytheism and idolatry of surrounding nations, did not allow Israel to think of the Spirit of God as a separate person or personality apart from YHWH. Rather their confession was "The Lord our God is one Lord" (Deut. 6:4, KJV).

The Hebrew word typically translated into English as "spirit" is *rûach* (*pneuma* in the Greek translation of the Old Testament). Basically, it means "wind." Possibly the first thing that strikes us as we study Old Testament usage of *rûach* is its quality of mystery and power. The *rûach* of God is never identical with the passions and longings of the people—although those people belong to God—and it is not generated *within* the community. It is not the product of any need or upward surge reaching out for its destiny. It was not born of any domestic spirit of togetherness.

God's *rûach* was a superhuman force that broke in from *without*. It was the supernatural invading the realm of the natural, sometimes causing havoc, at other times elusive, but always the source of extraordinary power that enabled a people, or some selected individual, to be lifted above natural capabilities. Hence, Joseph's ability to interpret Pharaoh's dream was attributed to this *rûach* (Gen. 41:38). The same entity stood behind Samson's power (Judges 13:25; 14:6, 19). Bezaleel, the skilled craftsman of the Tabernacle, was skilled because he was filled with the Spirit (Ex. 35:31). *Rûach* was responsible for the inspiration of the prophets (1 Kings 22:24; Isa. 61:1; Eze. 11:5; 2 Sam. 23:2; Micah 3:8); it gave the charisma of leadership to the judges of Israel (Judges 3:10; 11:29); it was the force behind the cherubim (Eze. 1:12, 20).

Probably *rûach* meant nothing more to the people of Israel than God in action, with emphasis on His power. And since the activity of God meant the presence of God, YHWH and His *rûach* blended together. Consequently, the Spirit was not thought of as something separate from God. This is illustrated in the prayer of Psalm 51, "Do not drive me from thy presence," with the parallel clause "or take thy holy spirit from me" (verse 11). Notice the similar parallelism of thought elsewhere: "Where can I escape from thy spirit? Where can I flee from thy presence?" (Ps. 139:7).

Isaiah 31:3 offers another interesting set of parallels: "The Egyptians are men, not God, their horses are flesh, not spirit." The contrast is not between matter and spirit. Isaiah is not saying that had the Egyptian horses been spirit they would not have been material, tangible. His point is that flesh coupled with man is weakness, whereas *rûach,* the bearer of which is God, means unlimited power. One expression describes the Egyptian strength, and the other that of the people who rely on God. It is through His *rûach* that God's personal will is being worked out "directed to a religious and moral end."[1]

The Bible opens (Gen. 1:2) by presenting the earth as a planet waste and void. As the scene is set to change this void into life, the Spirit of God is there "brooding" over the waters (KJV, margin). The Spirit of God plays a part in the act of Creation. While the word "brooding" is the same as that which describes the hovering of a bird (Deut. 32:11), it would, as one well-known scholar writes, be incorrect to see in this verse any ground for "the ancient and widespread belief in the primeval world-egg from which proceeded the earth, sky, sun, moon, and so forth; for this implies that the germ of world-life was in the egg. The biblical idea is different. That over which the Spirit broods is not potential life; it is chaos. The life is not in the chaos—it is in the Spirit (or breath, or wind)."[2]

The Spirit's brooding and the utterance of the words "Let there be light" are inseparably tied together in one almighty act, causing life to emerge out of chaos and nothingness, with no attempt made to explain or describe. Creating *out of nothing* is one of God's supreme qualities, whether in Creation or re-creation, in the initial making of this earth or in touching human beings who have lost contact with *life*. He causes life to emerge out of emptiness, chaos, and nothingness, and He does it by the "breath of his mouth" (Ps. 33:6, KJV).

Interestingly, Genesis 2:7 says that the Lord God breathed the breath of life into the nostrils of the first man. But Elihu, in the book of Job, says that "the Spirit of God made me," and then he blends this with Genesis 2:7 by adding that "the breath of the Almighty gave me life" (Job 33:4). The psalmist similarly says that the *rûach* of God is that wind which comes and kisses the earth to bring forth Creation (Ps. 33:6; 104:30, KJV). This underlines not only that the *rûach* means God in action but also that everything which has life derives its existence from this force.

On the concept of the Spirit as Re-creator, the prophecy of the dry bones in Ezekiel 37 is an interesting passage for study. The setting is the captivity of Israel. To the dejected and despondent people their nation certainly could have seemed like a heap of bleached bones in a barren valley. However, true to Himself, God promised to restore and redeem. But He would do it by His Spirit. "I will put my spirit into you and you shall live" (verse 14). The prophet offered a striking picture of the promised redemption to which the Old and New Testaments keep returning. Rot set in on the morning of humanity's sin, as it were. God responded by promising restoration. By His *rûach* He will achieve this.

It is and has always been a contradiction in terms to obstruct the workings of the Holy Spirit and still consider oneself eligible for restoration. Ellen G. White comments: "Through the agency of the *Holy Spirit* God designs that His image shall be restored in humanity, that a new and living principle of life shall be introduced into the minds that have become defiled by sin."[3]

"The *Spirit* re-creates, refines, and sanctifies human beings, fitting them to become members of the royal family, children of the heavenly King."[4]

Our choice in this matter is not in regard to the means or modes of the process of restoration, but in whether we shall be part of it or not.

The picture of the *rûach* that the Old Testament thus far presents to us is that of God's action in powerful and supernatural ways. God is at work, and the Spirit is the executive—the divine energy. A task is to be done, and the Spirit makes it possible. He is supremely functional. Nowhere does the *rûach* emerge as a kind of spiritual lollipop for personal and private enjoyment. The Holy Spirit in the Old Testament does not act as a personality separate from God, but neither is He in the New Testament conceived of as a gift separate from God. He is "not an influence at a distance from God Himself, and not a substance communicated to man."[5] The Holy Spirit is deity Himself.

The Old Testament has many references, some of which have already been mentioned, in which the Spirit is described as coming to rest on an individual. From this we can deduce that the Spirit functioned as a special link between God and the nation. As such, the Spirit was preeminently the Spirit of prophecy (Amos 3:7, 8; Micah 3:8, KJV). One highly respected commentary has shown how rabbinic traditions emphasized the Spirit as the Spirit of prophecy.

Whereas the Old Testament texts have "Spirit of God," the Targums—Aramaic paraphrases of the Hebrew Old Testament—render it consistently "Spirit of prophecy."[6]

The Spirit does not mean abstractions (such as the Spirit as a separate element). It was God breaking through to communicate Himself to humanity. But we have not lost sight of the Spirit as power, for in breaking through, God gives power both to understand and to respond. It may well be this that the recurring Hebrew parallelism of rûach with the "word of the Lord" (Ps. 33:6; cf. 2 Sam. 23:2, KJV) brings out in an emphasis on *communication*. The inevitable consequence of rejecting the Word of the Lord is that the Spirit of the Lord departs, as happened in Saul's case (1 Sam. 15:26; 16:14). There can be no tension between the Word of the Lord and the Spirit, for They are as indissolubly related as are the Spirit and Christ in New Testament thought (Rom. 8:9).

But as we approach the time of the Exile, we detect an unmistakable change of attitude toward the Spirit in Jewish communities. It is a shift that contains both hope and suspicion. As God's power and energy, the Spirit had, of course, always been present with Israel. But now He came increasingly to be thought of as that which is "yet to come." We find this eschatological emphasis particularly reflected in Ezekiel (Eze. 11:19; 37:1-14), but it can also be seen earlier (Isa. 44:1-5; Joel 2:28-32). The Spirit, now thought of as belonging to the age to come, was especially to accompany the Messiah (Isa. 11:1ff.).

This eschatological hope must be seen against the background of the setbacks that the nation was experiencing. The coming of the Messiah meant that God would make good on His promises, the fulfillment of which seemed so elusive at the time of Ezekiel. The anomaly between the shattered national hopes of the Jews and the belief that *their* God was the Almighty One was difficult for Israel to come to grips with.

In the trauma of their exilic state it was inevitable that the Jews should begin to ask questions about what went wrong, in spite of the danger of drawing wrong conclusions, for purely emotional reasons, when the event is so close at hand. But how could they step aside and look at it dispassionately?

The immediate questions would no doubt be What or who is to be blamed for the mess we now find ourselves in? How can things be set right? Which qualities must be cultivated and which shunned (particularly in the age after the Exile)? Increasingly, the answer came to be that things went wrong because the people had ignored the Torah and had begun listening to other voices. Hence the trend was set toward magnifying the law and cultivating suspicion of other voices. In such a climate the Spirit of prophecy was not welcomed. This is seen, among other things, in the fact that some exiles in Babylon became rather agitated that Jeremiah was still at large in Jerusalem, when he should have been imprisoned, which was the right treatment for "every madman who sets [himself] up as a prophet" (Jer. 29:26).

As decades passed after the return from the Exile, the increasing magnification of the Torah came at the expense of that "suspect and unstable breeze"—the Spirit of prophecy. The Torah came to be considered the last infallible revelation of God, and prophecy fell into disrepute.

One well-known authority on the subject writes: "In the third century B.C. the Law had come to be conceived as the final and supreme revelation of God. When once this idea of an inspired Law—adequate, infallible and valid for all time—had become an accepted dogma of Judaism, as it became in the post-Exilic period, there was no longer room for independent representatives of God appearing before men, such as the pre-Exilic prophets. God . . . had spoken His last and final word through the Law. . . . The

Law has not only assumed the function of the ancient pre-Exilic prophets, but it has also, as far as it lay in its power, made the revival of such prophecy impossible."[7]

Clearly, to claim to have the Spirit of prophecy in those days was risky business. No wonder so many writings appeared during these two or three centuries that were attributed to someone other than the persons who wrote them! One of the writings from this period indicates that the people believed that the law was not communicated by the Spirit, but by angels (*Jubilees* 1:27).

The people opted for the law, with its numerous sub-laws and interpretations because it was firm, specific, and tangible. The Spirit (of prophecy) appeared to them as too elusive. One could pause and reflect: Is this an inevitable pattern of legalism? Is legalism based on such a closed system that newness and freshness never slip through? Or, to put the same question more radically: If we continue to pray and long for the newness and freshness of the Spirit's latter rain, but fail to experience it, is it a reflection on a religious system operative in us individually that is immune to newness?

It is interesting to note that although the Qumran literature has much to say about the Spirit, it gives little prominence to His eschatological character. This may be surprising, considering the Qumran community's lively expectation of the end. It can be accounted for only in terms of the strong legalistic emphasis there. The *hope* of the coming of the Spirit is expressed in the main by prophets such as Joel, Isaiah, and Ezekiel.

One final point before we end our brief look at the Spirit in the Old Testament. We have noted that the concept *Word* is closely associated with the Spirit. So also is Wisdom. The concepts are not identical, but they are *functionally* close together. When we come to the New Testament, we find that Christ is not only identified with and closely linked to Wisdom and the Word, but also that Christ is the Word. This being so, remembering the Jewish hope that the renewed age would begin with the coming of the Messiah on whom the Spirit-to-come would rest, we would expect one of the obvious and outstanding qualities of the Messiah to be His Spirit-filledness. Spirit-filled He was, as we shall see from the next section. Yet, somewhat perplexingly, this was not a feature that Jesus or the early believers drew particular attention to. It is as though it was a secret, or part of the mystery that had to be kept hidden, at least for some time. Why was this so? Was being Spirit-filled a liability?

On that question we leave the Old Testament and turn to the New.

---

[1] Gerhard Kittel, *Theological Dictionary of the New Testament* (Grand Rapids: Wm. B. Eerdmans Pub. Co., 1968), Vol. VI, p. 365.

[2] C. K. Barrett, *The Holy Spirit and the Gospel Tradition* (London: SPCK, 1970), p. 18.

[3] Ellen G. White, *Testimonies to Ministers* (Mountain View, Calif.: Pacific Press Pub. Assn.), p. 378. (Italics supplied.)

[4] _______, *Gospel Workers* (Washington, D.C.: Review and Herald Pub. Assn., 1948), p. 287. (Italics supplied.)

[5] W. H. Griffith Thomas, *The Holy Spirit of God* (London: Church Book Room Press, Ltd., 1974), p. 16.

[6] Strack and Billerbeck, *Kommentaren zum neuen Testaments aus Midrash und Talmud,* vol. II, pp. 127f.

[7] R. H. Charles, *Apochrypha and Pseudepigrapha of the Old Testament* (London: Oxford Press, 1913), Vol. II, p. viii.

CHAPTER 2

The Holy Spirit in the Life of Jesus

The church has traditionally confessed that the Holy Spirit was the agent who united the human and the divine in the Incarnation. It may well be that in the Annunciation we find the Holy Spirit emerging as a distinct person or personality for the first time in the Bible. The angel said to Mary: "The Holy Spirit will come upon you" (Luke 1:35). The language is unmistakably clear, although we cannot make any useful reflection on what Mary understood of the Spirit on that occasion. She doubtless understood that the body of the Child that she would give birth to would be prepared by the Holy Spirit.

If we are asked to make a step-by-step rational explanation of what that means, words will fail us, because the message is not a rational statement or an explanation. It is, and will always remain, an in-faith confession. I know of no other way of accounting for this unique and absolute union of two natures in the one person of Jesus (a reversal of the Trinitarian formula of more persons in one nature) than by the story of the virgin birth with the Holy Spirit as cause. Without openness to the same Spirit, the mind "cannot hope to comprehend this subject."[1]

Of course, the record was written long after the experience of the Spirit on the day of Pentecost. However, one cannot read the passages without a feeling that the writers believed not only that Jesus was born of a virgin, but also that the cause was the same Spirit with whom they had had powerful and refreshing experiences at Pentecost and afterward.

Augustine, a church father, thought of the Holy Spirit as the "bond of love *(nexus amoris)*" between the Father and Son. Now, at the Incarnation, if we may bend Augustine's thought, the Spirit comes as minister of the union between God and humanity and thus becomes the highest expression of the "bond of love" that exists between the Godhead and humankind.

We must pause and answer the critic who says, "A woman conceiving at the intervention of a god? Such a story is not at all unique. There are a number of parallels to it in pagan myths."

Our answer comes from an a priori in-faith position. Of course, the critic similarly starts from another a priori position, although clearly not an in-faith one. The reason this out-of-faith assumption speculates that the stories in Matthew 1 and Luke 1 are best accounted for when seen as coming from a tradition similar to those of the cults is that it assumes a priori that miracles do not happen. From our in-faith perspective, we maintain that the Gospel accounts show some important differences from so-called parallels in pagan cults.

1. In contrast to pagan parallels, there is in the Gospel story a total absence of any male factor in the conception of Mary. Judaism and the Old Testament, to which the New Testament is so largely indebted for the concepts it draws on, generally recognized *rûach,* God's activity, as something *feminine* rather than as a personal demigod. (The Greek word for Spirit—*pneuma*—is neuter.) To them it was not natural, in the words of one scholar, "to think of the Spirit . . . as a male principle, capable (as Zeus and Apollo might have been supposed to be capable) of begetting children by mortal women."[2]

2. The moral tone in which the cultic stories are set, where no emphasis is laid on the moral purity or virginity of the mother, is totally foreign to the morality found in the Gospels and, for that matter, to the ethics of the whole New Testament.

The pagan stories at times describe the god as coming in a very personal way to the woman, and whether impregnation took place by regular sexual intercourse or was described with excessive magic as coming in the form of snakes, thunderbolts, or streams of gold (as in the stories of Apollo, Olympias, and Zeus), the women were often prostitutes (the so-called vestal virgins).

3. Whereas in the pagan stories the impregnation act is often by physical contact, the story of the virgin Mary contains nothing of that sort. On the contrary, notice the two verbs that the angel used in telling Mary what would happen. "The Holy Spirit *will come upon* you; and the power of the Most High *will overshadow* you" (Luke 1:35).

The Greek words for the verbs that we have italicized are *eperchomai* and *episkiazō*. C. K. Barrett makes the very important point that from their frequent usage in the Greek translation of the Old Testament, known as the Septuagint (LXX for short), they both denote "nonmaterial action" and are "never used of sexual intercourse,"[3] but on two occasions they are used in connection with *pneuma* (Num. 5:14, 30; Isa. 32:15).

Furthermore, the expression "come upon" *(eperchomai),* which is a Lucan favorite (eight of its 10 New Testament usages are by Luke), often has the context of coming with power or even violence (for instance, Luke 11:22). This is interesting, both with a view to what we have already said about the Old Testament's understanding of the Spirit as God's power breaking in from outside humanity, as well as to what we shall see at Pentecost and in the church immediately thereafter.

This would, I believe, allow us to agree with Barrett when he says that "the semidivine begetting of individuals by a god and a woman has no contact with the Matthaean and Lucan stories at the point where we are concerned with them, namely, the statement that the conception of Jesus was due not to an act of paternity on the part of a god, but to the supernatural and nonmaterial action of the Holy Spirit."[4]

If we are to look for an analogy to the story of the virgin birth by the power of the Holy Spirit, we shall find it not in the Greek myth stories but in the Old Testament story of Creation as found in Genesis. They meet at the point where both present the Spirit as Creator. Here, as at Creation (and as in Ezekiel's vision of the dry bones), the Spirit of the Almighty emerges as the one who creates *out of nothing.*

Not only was Jesus born of the Spirit, but also He "grew, and waxed strong in spirit, filled with wisdom" (Luke 2:40, KJV). The Spirit not only prepared His body, but also saw to it, very largely through the ministry of Mary,[5] that He was equipped to face the task ahead of Him. The so-called silent years of Jesus' life, far from being a vacuum, were a period when He was under the Holy Spirit's intensive tutelage.

Then came the hour of taking the public stage. Whatever else the baptism of Jesus may mean, this was the time when He emerged officially in terms of what He had come to be and to do. In this sense it was an inauguration. This was the moment when He came in fulfillment of the eschatological hopes of the Old Testament for a Spirit-anointed Messiah (Isa. 11:2; 61:1). At Jesus' baptism the Spirit descended from heaven as a dove, and a voice was heard saying: "Thou art my Son, my Beloved; on thee my favor rests" (Mark 1:11).

It is impossible for us to explain what happened, and

probably next to impossible for us to capture in detail the meaning and impact of that event. But enough is recorded to make it clear that both the descent of the dove and the heavenly voice must have brought eschatology alive to the Jewish mind that had come to understand and believe. It meant that they stood on the threshold of the new era with the Anointed One leading the way. The dove must have called to memory the Creation story of Genesis 1:2, with the Spirit "brooding" over the waters, or possibly even the dove sent out by Noah after the Flood (Gen. 8:8-12). It all contained the elements of a new creation—a new epoch in God's dealings. And the voice with its message was surely reminiscent of Psalm 2:7, which proclaims: "The Lord hath said unto me, Thou art my Son; this day have I begotten thee" (KJV); and Isaiah 42:1 declares: "Here is my servant, whom I uphold, my chosen one in whom I delight, I have bestowed my spirit upon him." To the Jewish mind that came to observe, understand, and believe, these points of contact must surely have been made. A sense of promise meeting its fulfillment was in the air.

There are those who have felt that this "hearing of a voice" followed a tradition that was already current in rabbinical literature, the so-called *bath qôl* revelations. The words literally mean "daughter of the voice" and refer to the hearing of a voice from heaven.[6] It was believed that when the Spirit of prophecy departed from Israel with the last prophet of the Old Testament an inferior means of revelation was given as a substitute for the Spirit-inspiration of the prophets. This substitute form of communication was called the *bath qôl*. The sound of the *bath qôl* was sometimes compared with the cry of a bird. Well, some would ask, is not this exactly what happened at the baptism of Jesus?

We would say emphatically "No!" What happened at the baptism of Jesus was no substitute for the Spirit; the

Spirit Himself was there. Rather, Jesus steps out of the tradition of the rabbis—if any of His contemporaries should have thought of Him in that classification—and into that of the prophets.[7] The age of the Messiah and the Spirit was about to begin.

One must be careful not to slip into the traps of an adoptionistic Christology by reading Mark 1:11 as merely an adoption formula. Jesus did not become at His baptism what He was not before, namely, the Only Begotten and the Beloved Son of God. He who was already the Beloved sent to become the Messiah was at His baptism inaugurated to begin the functions of that office and achieve that for which He came. Baptism is the moment of His anointing. Thus there is a sense in which He who is the Son becomes the Anointed One at His baptism, just as there is a sense in which He becomes the Deliverer at His resurrection (Acts 2:36; 13:33; Rom. 1:4) and High Priest at His ascension. At various stages in history Jesus assumed a fuller role of His Sonship and Messiahship. In the words of one writer: "It is not so much that Jesus became what He was not before, but that history became what it was not before."[8]

One must also guard against seeing the coming of the Spirit at Jesus' baptism merely as a sign of public installation as Messiah—as a kind of divine "imprimatur." It was an hour of power. At Jordan Jesus received a personal endowment of the Spirit that gave Him power and authority to undertake His Messianic mission (Acts 10:38). And as He shortly thereafter began His public ministry in Galilee, He did so "armed with the power of the Spirit" (Luke 4:14).

In some of the current Spirit-baptism discussions, cultivated in a climate of widespread charismatic longings in many churches, the baptismal experience of Jesus is being looked at in different ways, two of which we shall take note.

1. Certain Pentecostals and neo-Pentecostals argue that *if* it was necessary for Jesus, who had received a su-

pernatural "natural" birth from above through the power of the Holy Spirit, to experience an additional blessing and filling of the Spirit at baptism in order to be equipped for the task ahead of Him, *how much more* should Christians receive, and need to receive, a special Spirit-baptism after their initial birth from above, after conversion.

2. Another reaction is that which holds that the baptism of John with which Jesus was baptized stands in a direct causal relationship to the descent of the Holy Spirit upon Him. This argument is used to assert that baptism in water is ipso facto the means by which the Holy Spirit comes into one's life. This is a heavily sacramental understanding of baptism.

On the surface it might appear that the Pentecostals have a case. From the first of the two viewpoints it is quite clear that the descent of the Holy Spirit at Jesus' baptism was unique in His life, and that therefore there is a sense in which one can speak of His baptism as a "Spirit-baptism," although the Spirit was no alien in His life prior to that. In one sense the Spirit did come as a "later experience" to Him, although no one will doubt His genuineness and commitment before that experience. Clearly this descent of the Spirit was to equip Him for the life and mission that lay ahead. Of course, Jesus was a Spirit-filled man (John 3:34; Acts 10:38). But do the Pentecostals, and those who think as they do, really have support here for their Spirit-baptism teaching?

The failure of the Pentecostals' argument here rests basically on the same faulty hermeneutics that they use when interpreting Spirit-experiences recorded elsewhere in the New Testament, especially in the book of Acts. They do not seem to appreciate the fact that salvation history is a process—an onward movement that goes through stages *that are not repeatable.* Each stage introduces a new epoch and a wider dimension of the whole process of God restoring humanity to Himself, whether it be that of Jesus' baptism, His ascension, Pentecost, or Samaria and Ephesus (or, for that matter, 1844). They fail to see that we cannot turn time back to these previous events and relive the experiences of those for whom the events were yet to come.

There is no parallel between the bestowal of the Spirit on Jesus at His baptism and the "second blessing" (or "delayed honeymoon") quest of Pentecostalism, because in the life of Jesus what happened at the Jordan was not second to anything. It was an inaugural event. It began the Messianic age. It initiated Jesus into the Messianic office. It was a totally unique experience and lacks parallels in anyone's Christian experience.

Now to the second viewpoint. Was there a direct causal relationship between the baptism of John, which Jesus experienced, and the descent of the Spirit? If there was, what happened to the many others who were similarly baptized by John? Why do the records not speak of them as having received the Spirit? As a matter of fact, the opposite would appear to be the case. John's baptism was not the context for discernible Spirit experiences. (See Paul's encounter at Ephesus in Acts 19. We will return for a fuller discussion of this point later.)

But even if there were a causal relationship between Jesus' baptism and the descent of the Spirit, which we have just said we cannot find, what could this possibly tell us about the relationship between Christian baptism (Matt. 28:18, 19; Acts 2:38) and the gift of the Holy Spirit? John's message was not as complete as the message that Jesus preached. But John was a forerunner in that he and his ministry pointed forward to that which was to come. In this sense his baptism was both symbolic and prophetic. It had a compelling urgency behind it because John believed that time was very short and that the people must get ready to meet the kingdom, which was about to break in on them. The King was about to come and open a new future.

John's baptism was an expression of repentance, a willingness to renounce the past and prepare to receive the Messianic age with the ethical and spiritual consequences of a new kind of life.

Jesus came to the Jordan River, and in the true prophetic tradition of the Old Testament identified Himself with His people and their sins (Rom. 8:29; Heb. 2:17).[9] As the second Adam, He was *the* representative human. He submitted to the will of God (Matt. 3:15) and committed Himself to fulfill the mission He had been sent to do. It was in response to these three—identification with the people, submission to God's will, and loyalty to His mission—that the Spirit was given, the voice was heard, and the Messianic age was inaugurated.

Consequently, if we are going to talk about any causal relationship in connection with the descent of the Holy Spirit on Jesus at His baptism, it will have to be tied to Jesus' state of mind and the decision He had made, rather than to the outward water baptism of John, although His participation in it came as an expression of what had been going on in His mind and the decision He had made. To suggest any other kind of causal relationship would simply be a reading back into the experience the type of arguments that the church of the third and fourth centuries came to accept, which made baptism the means of forgiveness and which in itself effected an infusion of grace from above. (We recognize, however, that the Church Fathers were themselves inconsistent, both among themselves and individually, in their views of what function baptism had, as Professor Lampe has shown in a useful study of this subject.)[10] Without denying that baptism can and ought to be a genuine meeting place between believers and their God—a point in one's experience when one actually receives much from God—such a heavy sacramentalistic view of Christian baptism is unwarranted. Clearly, there is no ground at all for looking at the baptism of Jesus and the accompanying descent of the Holy Spirit from this kind of causal point of view.

If the experience of Jesus at the Jordan teaches us anything about Spirit baptism as a believer might meet it, it surely must be that the gift of the Spirit is inseparably tied to what goes on in one's mind. Where there is no repentance, no submission, no commitment, and no willingness to accept the consequences of living a life in harmony with the kingdom, no external rites whatsoever will bestow the gift. Neither will enthusiastic spiritual pressure groups, under the umbrella of charismatic renewal, do this, although the display of enthusiasm is at times rather overwhelming.

All three Synoptists tell us that after His baptism Jesus was led into the wilderness to face the tempter (Matt. 4:1-11; Mark 1:12, 13; Luke 4:2-13). All three make the point that it was the Spirit who led Him there. It is easy to misread the account in such a way that one ends up with distortions of what really happened. It would be misleading to see this event as something prearranged by the Spirit as a test of strength between the newly appointed Messiah and His archenemy. Jesus' reasons for going to the desert were totally different from the design of the tempter who met Him there.

Similarly, it would be wrong to read into this story the idea that the Spirit led Jesus particularly during the next few turbulent weeks, when He would be stretched to His absolute limit, after which, if He came through intact, He would be able to manage on His own.

Jesus did not go into the arena to meet a scheduled event. "He did not invite temptation."[11] He went there to pray and to contemplate the mission ahead of Him.

It seems that the Synoptists wish to say that when Jesus

began His years of ministry He did so under the leadership of the Holy Spirit and that when He emerged as conqueror 40 days later He did so because of the presence of the Holy Spirit. The focal point in their record is the presentation of Jesus as the man *in whom the Spirit is,* and of victory as the outcome of Spirit-filledness. Surely that is a point that the believer cannot afford to overlook.

Of course, Jesus was not discharged into the world on His own after this successful encounter with the evil one. His victory in the wilderness was by the Spirit. And the Gospel of Mark particularly emphasizes that it was by the same Spirit He continued His defeat of the same Beelzebub by casting out evil and unclean spirits. This was not achieved in the name of His own divine Sonship, but in the name of the Holy Spirit. Jesus, as the Messiah, came as the bearer of the Holy Spirit. An early Jewish-Christian thought, preserved for us in Jerome's commentary on the prophecy of Isaiah 11:1, may be an interesting comment on what we are trying to say: "It came to pass that when the Lord had ascended from the water the whole fountain of the Holy Spirit descended and rested upon him, and said to him, 'My Son, in all the prophets I looked for thee, that thou mightest come and I might rest in thee; for thou art my Son, my first-born, who art king for evermore.' "[12]

Jesus emerges in the Gospels as the one who has conquered the devil and who, in His ministry, continues to conquer him and his demons. He is capable of holding conversations with these evil spirits, and they recognize Him as their conqueror (Mark 3:11; 5:7-13; 9:25). His mastery over them was a sign of God's power and of the kingdom. "If it is by the Spirit of God that I drive out the devils, then be sure the kingdom of God has already come upon you" (Matt. 12:28).

And yet, returning to the point on which we closed our discussion of the Spirit in the Old Testament, we are perplexed by the fact that Jesus, who as Messiah came as the peculiar bearer of the Holy Spirit, somehow seems reluctant to publicize His Spirit-filled quality in a way that cannot satisfactorily be put down to humility. There is no doubt that the Spirit rested on Him "without measure." The extent to which the Spirit was present in His life and ministry cannot be measured by the number of texts or statements we find explicitly referring to the Spirit. He was endowed with charismatic gifts and was, therefore, one whom the label "pneumatic" really fit.

As one writer observes, when Jesus healed or cast out devils He acted "not as a doctor who treats disease, but as a 'pneumatic' man who commands it."[13] The Spirit of prophecy rests on Him as He makes predictions about both His own fate and that of Jerusalem. He is able to read the hidden secrets of the heart. And yet He conspicuously avoids calling attention to His Spirit-filledness. He never mentions His baptism (Mark 10:38ff. and Luke 12:50 refer to another experience). And when He heals people or casts out devils, He is more likely than not to tell those involved to keep it secret. We cannot help asking, Why?

There are some specific reasons for the silence.

Note first the label "pneumatic." It seems to be one that Jesus wanted to avoid. There were a lot of bogus pneumatics around, particularly in the Hellenistic world, who were known for their bizarre activities. They were a flash in the pan. They left no lasting impact behind. We meet some of them in the book of Acts—for example, Simon Magus (8:9-24), Elymas (13:6-12), and the seven sons of Sceva (19:14). The label had a slurred and pejorative meaning, and if there was anything Jesus had to avoid, it was to allow anyone to think of Him as coming in that kind of tradition.

Of "pneumatic" individuals there were many. But Jesus was different, and it was vitally important that He come across to His community, His followers, and His posterity as one of a kind. He could not be relegated to an already-existing category, even by the unsympathetic. He was *the* Christ, *the* promised Messiah, and for such there was no tradition. Neither did He start a "Christ-tradition" in which others since have come. He was unique.

Another point is that He was equally reluctant to publicize on the street corners that He was the Messiah. Surely a reason for this is that He did not fit into the slot that Judaism had prepared for its Messiah. The program He had to carry through in His ministry to provide the foundation on which the church could stand and grow was such that prudence was the wiser course. To place Himself prematurely in the arena of controversy would have made it all the more difficult for Him to continue His ministry. But this was also the reason He did not stress the line of relationship between Himself and the Spirit: He could not have done so without declaring His Messiahship about which it was His intention to be quiet.

But both the Spirit-filledness and Messiahship of Jesus discreetly come out in His life and are discernible to the eyes and ears of faith. Beyond the "charismatic" action of Jesus and what He said about Himself, His whole teaching concerning the kingdom was about the ministry of the Spirit—"not the Spirit substantially or in Itself, but functionally and in the effects It will have."[14]

The ministry of the Spirit is to fashion the kingdom as the community of faith. And although He was present with Jesus without measure, and no doubt in some measure with His immediate followers, His coming in power to the community of faith was yet to come—after Jesus had been glorified. "The Spirit had not yet been given, because Jesus had not yet been glorified" (John 7:39).

We might note a third point: Just as the doctrine of the Spirit in the Old Testament came to have an eschatological feature associated with the coming Messiah, so after the Messiah had been anointed, the Spirit remained eschatological. The community of faith could really understand the Spirit and His ministry only after Jesus had been glorified (John 7:39), because it was those very things—the cross and Resurrection, the Ascension and glorification, and Christ's heavenly ministry—that the Spirit had come to make meaningful to the world in the end-time.

According to the context of John 7:38ff., in which Jesus is recorded as speaking about "streams of living water," He was speaking about the Holy Spirit, which His disciples could not receive until after His glorification. Consequently, it would have been impossible for the followers of Jesus, even His closest 12, to have understood the peculiar meaning of Jesus Christ as the "bearer of the Holy Spirit." It can be understood only from a post-Pentecost position.

It is important to recognize that the whole process of understanding is enormously conditioned by events in history and *our participation* in them. Did not Jesus Himself make the point that there were many more things He would like to have told His disciples that they were not in a position to receive then, but which they would be able to receive after the Spirit had come? (See John 16:12, 13.)

---

[1] Ellen G. White, "The Word Made Flesh," in *Review and Herald,* Apr. 5, 1906.

[2] C. K. Barrett, *The Holy Spirit and the Gospel Tradition,* p. 23.

[3] *Ibid.,* p. 7.

[4] *Ibid.,* p. 8.

[5] Ellen G. White, *The Desire of Ages* (Mountain View, Calif.: Pacific Press Pub. Assn.), pp. 69f.

[6] Strack and Billerbeck, *Kommentaren zum neuen Testaments aus Midrash und Talmud,* Vol. I, pp. 125-128.

[7] Barrett, p. 40.

[8] J. G. Dunn, *Baptism in the Holy Spirit* (Naperville, Ill.: Alec R. Allenson, Inc.), p. 29.

[9] See White, *The Desire of Ages,* p. 40.

[10] G. W. Lampe, *The Seal of the Spirit* (London: SPCK, 1967).

[11] White, *The Desire of Ages,* p. 114.

[12] This comment, preserved for us by Jerome, comes from the noncanonical "Gospel according to the Hebrews," which is otherwise lost.

[13] Barrett, p. 114.

[14] J. C. Haughey, *The Conspiracy of God: The Holy Spirit in Men* (New York, Doubleday & Co., Inc., 1973), p. 15.

CHAPTER 3

The Place of the Holy Spirit in the Teachings of Jesus

John the Baptist spoke prophetically when he said of Jesus that He would "baptize . . . with the Holy Spirit and with fire" (Matt. 3:11; Luke 3:16). Even though, following the baptism of Jesus, John received an assurance that this was the Messiah,[1] he could not have understood the full meaning of the prophetic statement he made. Again, it requires a post-Pentecost Christian experience to give specific content to those words, and even then it may be far from clear what "fire" means.

William Barclay's suggestion that fire refers to the warmth, illumination, and purification of the entry of Jesus into one's heart seems vague. Some have thought that it may refer to the hardships and persecutions that Christians will have to face as a consequence of their faith—this was probably the way many early Christians understood it. Others saw it as a reference to the day of judgment, reflecting Old Testament and Jewish thoughts (Isa. 5:24; Dan. 7:9, 10; Mal. 4:1f.; 3:1-4, together with a Qumran hymn [1QH 3:28ff.] describing the same). Again, others understood it as simply a further reference to the Holy Spirit and His work.

But why must we choose among them? Maybe John the Baptist merely wanted to confess that the One who stood before them was the Messiah and that the Holy

Spirit rested on Him. John was now acknowledging with humility that his own ministry was but preparatory, that of a forerunner.

As we have already noted, there is a marked lack of Spirit references in the teachings of Jesus, and we have suggested reasons that this is so. But we must again emphasize that it is much too superficial and inadequate to measure Spirit-content in the teachings and sayings of Jesus by the number of explicit references. Reading by the eyes of faith through the experience of Pentecost, it is not difficult to find the Holy Spirit in the teachings of Jesus.

Nevertheless, as far as the Synoptics go, we have only a handful of explicit references. (Those referring to sin against the Holy Spirit—Matthew 12:31, 32; Mark 3:28, 29; Luke 12:10—will be examined separately.) There is the assurance Jesus gave His disciples that the Spirit would aid their speech in days of difficulties when proclaiming the gospel of the kingdom (Matt. 10:18-20; Mark 13:11; Luke 12:11, 12).

In connection with this promise of the Spirit we must not overlook an invaluable parallel saying of Jesus. He says that under these persecutions and difficulties *"I myself* will give you power of utterance" (Luke 21:15). The point is that the Spirit and Jesus are inextricably linked. The Spirit does not communicate except in communicating Jesus Christ as Lord and Saviour. In this sense the Spirit is both the gift and the giver: the gift of the ascended and glorified Lord, and the giver who brings this Lord to us. Thus Jesus was able to say at one moment: "You will not always have me" (Matt. 26:11) and a few days later: "Be assured, I am with you always, to the end of time" (Matt. 28:20). The logical conclusion of this is that any spirit-enthusiasm which fails to communicate Christ, what He stood for, and what discipleship means is of a spirit other than the one Jesus promised.

In another instance Jesus referred to David as being "inspired by the Holy Spirit" (Mark 12:36), and He quotes from the opening of Psalm 110. However, Luke, in his parallel section (Luke 20:41, 42), does not specifically attribute this saying of David to the action of the Spirit. But there is no ground for reading anything about Luke's understanding of the Spirit into that omission, for in another instance in which Matthew refers to the "good things" that the Father will send (Matt. 7:11), Luke specifically says "the Holy Spirit" (Luke 11:13). Additionally, Luke's record of some of the parting words of Jesus was: "I am sending upon you my Father's promised gift; so stay here in this city until you are armed with the power from above" (Luke 24:49). It is very clear that He here refers to the Holy Spirit and Pentecost.

And then, of course, there is the gospel commission (Matt. 28:19), which is clearly Trinitarian.

The few statements made by Jesus about the Holy Spirit make clear that the Spirit is to come as a specific gift. Consequently, the presence of the Spirit is not to be confused with something highly subjective, such as a devotional frame of mind with a pietistic or enthusiastic slant. He is inextricably associated with the person of Jesus and His mission. He is not to be conceived of as separate or something to be sought for *His own sake*. When He comes He will give power to witness and to speak in times of difficulty. The Holy Spirit is very functional. There is clearly no suggestion that He is something to be cultivated or "enjoyed" as a private in-group "thing."

We now turn to the Gospel of John to find whether our impression is confirmed, changed, or enlarged.

The fourth Gospel is more devotionally reflective in nature than the other three. While John's Gospel is important to an understanding of the Spirit in general, it is especially so to an understanding of the "Spirit-baptism." If individuals are not prepared to accept such "Spirit-baptism" as a separate experience, they are going to have to come to grips with some issues raised by this Gospel interpreted by some as supporting it.

The relatively late date of John's Gospel—we would accept it as having been written by John the apostle at the close of the first century—has led many scholars to insist that what John wrote about the Spirit came not from the authentic teaching of Jesus, but from the belief and *kērygma* (preaching) of the church. It is pointed out that when John wrote his Gospel, the church had outlived much of the eschatological tension that was so real during the first few decades after Christ's ascension.

There is little doubt that the first Christians believed that the ascended Lord would return very soon, probably in their own lifetime, as suggested by Paul (1 Thess. 5:1-11; 2 Thess. 2:1-12). But when John wrote his Gospel, Paul had been dead for three decades, and the Lord had not yet come back. This situation may have come as a real shock to those first-generation believers who were still alive. Confronted with that situation, some scholars argue that the church and John simply woke up to the facts of life and began to wonder seriously whether they had not, in fact, completely misunderstood eschatology. According to the conjecture of some of these critics, maybe the promised return of the Lord was fulfilled in the coming of the Holy Spirit in the minds of these early Christians. Many of these scholars feel that John wrote his Gospel to reinterpret eschatology as the present experience of the Spirit.

Much of this conjecture is clearly of no use to us. True, the early believers expected the Lord to return quickly—most likely during their own lifetime. They were no doubt disappointed as decades passed and many were laid to rest, and the Lord did not come. But there is nothing to suggest that an erosion of belief set in, that they did such an about-face as to hold that their eschatology had been completely mistaken, and that, consequently, the sayings of Jesus had to be rewritten so as to fit the actual situation. This is a problem created by some modern scholars and read back into the mind of the community of John's day.

What is clear, however, is that John looks at the events and sayings of Jesus from a much greater distance than the other New Testament writers, and he does so with a posture of meditation and devotion. He is reflective in his writing. This quite obviously affects his selection of material and the way he puts it in writing.

Note, therefore: (a) John wrote with a greater span of time between himself and the actual events than did the other Gospel writers, and he did so with marked devotional reflections; and (b) he had access to at least some of the other Gospels when he wrote; we would understand that he did not merely want to repeat what they had already said.

The Gospels complement one another in their emphases. John is the last writer to contribute to the making of New Testament theology. When he wrote, Paul's impact on the Christian community had already been made, the gospel had been widely proclaimed, and churches had been established, effecting considerable organizational structure. It is from this kind of position in history that John sat down and reflected on the events surrounding the life of Jesus Christ.

Consequently, time, in the biographical sense of separating happenings with care and measuring the distance between events that obviously were separate when they happened, was not foremost in his mind. He may have felt that the other Gospel writers had already done that. Obviously, he did not violate time so as to give the wrong picture of what happened (his Gospel is invaluable when it comes to reconstructing the chronology of Jesus' ministry).

But it is important to understand that his concern was not with stringing out events as such with the right measured distance between them. Rather, his urgent aim was to underline that the Jesus of history is the Christ of salvation. History to John was first and foremost the *history of salvation.* He wished to say that the One at the center of this history is both God and man.

With this in mind John reflected on the meaning of the events surrounding Jesus Christ. As he did so, events that were separate when they happened, in the sense that time elapsed between them, were allowed to flow together and become one, because in terms of salvation-history he felt that they belonged together and were really one event.

There is nothing strange in this approach. Maybe our own personal salvation experience can illustrate what we mean: the first meeting we attended, feeling the message stirring in our soul, a further period of study accompanied by a growth in belief, the moment of repentance, and a definite decision for Christ climaxed by baptism. Although all these events are strung out over a period of weeks and possibly months—even years—they belong together as one. Together they make up a personal conversion/regeneration experience. They mark a point of entry into God's kingdom.

Although my own actual decision came at 9:00 p.m. one Friday evening, it is clear to me today as I look back that what happened that evening was possible only because of what had gone before. Furthermore, it would not have been a decision had it not led to my public witness in baptism some two months later.

In his Gospel, John was doing something akin to that. Looking back on the life of Jesus, he saw, from the perspective of more than half a century, events blending or dovetailing into one another, although obviously they had been spread out during a period of weeks.

This pattern of John's can be seen particularly in what

he said about the Spirit. On this subject he wished to make one main point, namely, that the gift of the Spirit is the gift of the *ascended* Lord, that is, after His glorification (John 7:37-39). John used the same word (*doxazein,* "to glorify") in speaking about Christ's death (John 12:23ff. and 13:31) as well as in speaking about the Ascension, with the resultant gift of the Spirit (John 7:39; 12:16; 17:5). The idea of the blending together of events is similarly seen in chapter 6, verses 62 and following, where the Ascension dovetails into the ministry of the Holy Spirit.

What we are saying is that, from John's point of view 60 years afterward, together the events of those 50 days between Passover and Pentecost made up the finale of that particular act in Christ's ministry, after which He ascended to begin His ministry above. As such they belong together and can be viewed as one. To John the gift of the Spirit is the gift of the Exalted One. It is the immediate consequence of the Ascension. Again, we see that time, in the sense of spacing things out with the proper distance between, was not a main concern for John.

Furthermore, what John wanted to bring out clearly in writing the story of Jesus, particularly in His farewell discourses, is that the Holy Spirit and Jesus Christ are inseparably united in Their work. The ministry of the Comforter is a direct continuity of the work Jesus did while here on earth, just as Jesus' ministry carried on the Father's work. As the Father came to humanity in Christ, so Christ comes to believers in the ministry of the Spirit (cf. John 8:42; 13:3; 15:26; 16:27).

Jesus could hardly have underlined this continuity more strongly than when He said, having emphasized that He would send them "another Comforter," "I will not leave you comfortless: I will come to you" (John 14:18, KJV), meaning that He would be present with the believers through the ministry of the Spirit.

However, while underlining continuity on the one hand, on the other John appears eager to bring out that Jesus emphasized a difference, or personal distinction, between Himself and the Spirit. In order to bring out both *identity* and *difference,* Jesus deliberately used the expression "Comforter" on four occasions in His farewell discourses (verses 16, 26; 15:26; 16:7, KJV). He thus underlined the fact that the coming Holy Spirit would continue the work of "Comforter" that He Himself had already been doing for three and a half years in teaching, encouraging, rebuking, and judging. He also designated the coming One as "another," clearly showing Him to be Someone other than Himself.

It would be a distortion to see the Spirit's coming as that of Christ who had merely turned a few degrees to show another side of Himself. The promised return of the Lord is still yet to come even after the Comforter has come. The only valid way to understand the promise of the coming of another Comforter is in the bestowal of the Holy Spirit on the day of Pentecost. He came then as a permanent and resident gift to the community of faith.

While John's Gospel is clear about the close link between Jesus Christ and the Holy Spirit, it raises points that are problems to some with reference to the gift of the Spirit. Scholars and "Spirit-enthusiasts" have in their different ways bent John's thoughts and the words of Jesus beyond what is justified. We must examine some of the points that are made.

1. John 20:22 says: "Then he breathed on them, saying, 'Receive the Holy Spirit!'" This statement is found only in John. From the context, one receives the impression that the resurrection and bestowal of the Holy Spirit came on the same day. Scholars are divided as to what to make of it. Some take the position that there is a clear tension between Luke's Pentecost in Acts 2 and that of John here. They sug-

gest that (a) John's timing is correct, that Luke's account is a part of "produced" history, and that consequently Acts 2 does not correspond with the actual time of the event; or (b) since John allowed events that belonged together to blend, in verse 22 he makes a compact statement containing both the Resurrection, Ascension, and gift of the Spirit, because he felt that they really did belong together, although, of course, they were spread out over some 50 days.

Without becoming carried away by conjectures and high-flung speculations, we find the first interpretation clearly unacceptable, but the second one does not offer much help either. As we read the verse in question in context, we cannot escape the feeling that John was writing about something very private and personal between the resurrected Lord and His inner circle "late that Sunday evening" (John 20:19). John 20:22 is something quite different from Acts 2.

With beauty and clarity Ellen G. White gives us a description of the scene on that Sunday evening, which helps us reconstruct the picture.[2] After Jesus had died on the cross the disciples were mentally and emotionally bewildered. They did not understand His Messiahship and had no concept of His resurrection. Then into their midst came Jesus. He breathed the Spirit on them, which helped them sort out their confused thinking so that despair gave way to hope. In their previous state they were in no condition to go out and witness. Then, as now, it was only the Spirit, bestowed by the resurrected Lord, who could lift the fog and help the disciples to understand the meaning of discipleship. Jesus wanted His followers to understand, as must we to whom the finishing task is given, "that without the Holy Spirit this work could not be accomplished."[3] Far from John 20:22 and Acts 2 being "confused history," what happened late that Sunday evening must be understood as preliminary to Pentecost.

But, some will say, having made that point, have you not now gotten yourself into an even greater problem? Are you in agreement with the Pentecostals, who argue that John 20:22 describes the moment of regeneration for the disciples and that Pentecost six or seven weeks later came as the actual hour of baptism in the Spirit? *And,* furthermore, do you say that John 20:22 constitutes a pattern for Christian experience, namely, that after the conversion/regeneration experience one should seek the "second blessing," which is the baptism in the Spirit?

No!

Unfortunately many people whose main concern is to receive what they call "Spirit-baptism" are pursuing their goal, as already noted, while employing faulty biblical hermeneutics. They fail to recognize that you cannot turn back the clock and that there are certain events in history that are not repeatable. The Crucifixion, Resurrection, Ascension, and Pentecost are in the past. We cannot individually relive the experiences of those connected with the events, whose lives spanned the time immediately before, during, and after them. One cannot in this sense unwind history.

What we are saying is that in John 20:22 we learn that Jesus did something special for His disciples *then.* Let us not forget: They went through the very gradual stages of moving away from their Jewish traditions; they had lived for three and a half years with One whom they understood only in part; and they went through the trauma of Calvary for which, in spite of all that Jesus had said to them, they were unprepared. Then came the first report of His resurrection.

The disciples, then, lived when the heart of the salvation drama was being unfolded before them in *separate experiences.* Today we can look back on the whole as a completed experience. It is impossible for us now to turn around and say that we today must experience the same sequence of events, understanding, and emotional trauma must be experienced by us. As one writer puts it: "A set of experiences whose order and depth was determined by an utterly unique and unrepeatable set of events (those from Bethlehem to Pentecost) cannot be the pattern for the regular experience of conversion and Christian growth after Pentecost."[4]

2. One of the most important passages on the Spirit in the fourth Gospel is chapter 3, verses 5ff., which say in part: "No one can enter the kingdom of God without being born from water and spirit." Those words are important in the main because to enter God's kingdom and to have assurance about it is what every earnest seeker after truth wants.

But the wording of the text is such that it seems to imply what some may find difficult to accept—that the birth "from water" and "spirit" are two different things, or if not, that birth "from water" (a reference to baptism) in itself assures one entry into God's kingdom. We have not been brought up on that kind of sacramentalism. Let us examine what John says.

Jesus is speaking to Nicodemus, and what He here calls "born from water and spirit" He calls "born over again" in verse 3. Jesus nowhere indicated that He shared the kind of sacramental understanding of either baptism or the Lord's Supper that Roman Catholics and some Protestants have come to hold. The elements used in these ordinances, entirely apart from the believer's faculties for responding in faith, do not impart life.

Chapters 6 and 7 of John are a valuable commentary on what Jesus meant in chapter 3, verse 5, and should be read before we proceed further. Jesus speaks about Himself as the Bread of Life and Water of Life, and about hungering and thirsting as acts of believing (John 6:35, 40, 47, 48, 51, 53-58, 64; 7:38, 39). He makes at least two points. First, belief must be centered in Jesus Christ the Incarnate, who was made in order to die. Second, eternal life comes through the Spirit, the gift of the glorified Lord. But above all, Jesus is Himself the source of life. There are no substitutes (including the Eucharistic elements) for Him.

Now let's return to the question of whether birth "of water" and "of spirit" are one and the same, or different things. In John's Gospel the metaphor of water carries a distinctly symbolic meaning. In the first half, particularly, the idea of cleansing is strongly brought out. The first public act of Jesus was to cleanse the Temple (John 2:12ff.). He is making a new temple in which a new kind of worshiper will worship God "in spirit and in truth" (John 4:24), a point that was brought clearly home to both Nicodemus and the woman at the well.

Coupled with the concept of cleansing *in order to make something new* is the idea of water (John 3:5ff.; 4:1ff., 14, 15; 5:3ff.). Water symbolized birth (to Nicodemus) as well as bounty (to the woman at the well). Then there was the preaching of John, which culminated in water-baptism. Water was used for purification by the priests at the Temple, and it was employed extensively as a symbol of purification in certain Jewish sectarian communities. All this made water an element full of symbolic meaning for the Jews—part of the cultural air they breathed.

Jesus came to inaugurate a new kingdom and a new age. Entrance into this kingdom and participation in this age were marked by the washing of regeneration and the newness ministered by the Holy Spirit. The idea of water becomes merged with the expression "Spirit" to signify purification, initiation, and newness. These, then—water and Spirit, purification and newness—jointly usher the believer into the new kingdom. They certainly do not signify two different stages of entry, or for that matter, two different things. As Jesus spoke He used water as a metaphor for the Spirit.[5]

We shall not linger at this point on the question of

whether water-baptism and Spirit-baptism are identical or different, and, if different, whether it is a time and space problem or a fundamental difference in meaning that separates them. We have already indicated the direction in which our answer will go, but we shall return to it later. Our final answer will depend on how we really understand Christian baptism.

Suffice it to say at this point that in the third chapter of John Jesus brings out a number of contrasting and complementary expressions intended to explain what He meant by "born from water and spirit" in verse 5. This expression is parallel to "to spirit" (verse 6) and "born over again" (verse 3), as well as "from above" or "from heaven" (verse 31). The contrast to this birth is that which is "of the flesh" (verse 6, KJV) and "from the earth" (verse 31).

That which is of the Spirit is clearly from above and radically different from anything that comes "from below." Whatever else it may mean, it means first and foremost that birth in or of the Spirit is of a totally different nature than anything generated or induced by self or society. It is distinctly said to be "from above."

3. Jesus said to the woman at the well, "God is spirit, and those who worship him must worship in spirit and in truth" (John 4:24). This statement has led some to see a universalism of the Spirit in which all sincere seekers of truth are such because of the Spirit's presence and leading. The criterion is to be found in the sincerity of one's search. Some scholars hold the Spirit to be so diffused that He is taken to be present and operative in the truth-quest of all religious systems of the world.[6] While resisting, on the one hand, any suggestion that the Holy Spirit is the property of Christianity—that would surely be to put the cart before the horse, since Christianity is maintained by Him—He is greater than it and cannot be contained by any organization or structure.

We cannot, on the other hand, take the way of those

whose sympathy toward non-Christian religions has sadly infringed their biblical exegesis. Professor Moule observed once: "To generalise the Holy Spirit and use the term to denote God's activity anywhere and everywhere, is to miss the biblical theme of election for service, and to ignore God's strange way of particularising in order to universalise."[7]

Jesus was looking into the immediate future and saw how vulnerable persons would become if their worship had to be tied to one particular location or environment. He especially had in view what would befall Jerusalem a few years later. And so in John 4:24 He emphasized that the gift of the Spirit to those who believe on Jesus Christ would make genuine worship possible anywhere. The worship of God transcends physical premises, as God's children continually discover in difficult days of war and persecution. It is a spiritual necessity for all believers to learn to "sing the Lord's song in a foreign land" (Ps. 137:4).

We must not forget that "spirit" in John 4:24 refers to the divine Gift, not to an attitude of the human mind, just as "truth" in the same text is not a reference to human intention or sincerity. Both terms refer to God as revealed in Jesus Christ and as coming to us afresh in the ministry of the Holy Spirit. Were it not for the Spirit, Jesus would disappear into the mist of the past. The Spirit makes Him Emmanuel—"God with us." It is the Spirit who makes this promise of Jesus possible: "Anyone who loves me will heed what I say; then my Father will love him, and we will come to him and make our dwelling with him" (John 14:23). In this sense the Holy Spirit universalizes Jesus. He makes Christ transcend time and space.

Before leaving this section we should reflect for a moment on the meaning of *Paraklete* (Comforter), by which the Spirit-then-to-come is described in John's Gospel. We cannot find any English word that covers its meaning completely. The word tells something about His function and relationship to humankind. It means basically "One called alongside to help," and could, therefore, be translated Helper, Comforter, Intercessor, Teacher, Companion. But it has also a legal connotation and could be either a defense counsel or a prosecutor, and with reference to the Holy Spirit, probably both.

The work of the Spirit is not of a different order from that of Jesus. As the Lord taught His disciples the truth about Himself (John 14:6, 16-18), so will the Spirit of truth teach, guide, and correct (John 15:26; 16:13). The Spirit does not speak for Himself. His function is the same as that of Jesus in the Gospels, namely, to reveal (cf. John 16:13; 5:19). As the Son revealed the Father, so the Spirit is to reveal the Son (John 15:26). He would teach and guide disciples into all truth, both by recalling what Jesus had already made clear and by making clear to their understanding what they were not ready to understand while Jesus was still among them (John 14:26; 16:12). And it is by virtue of the power and ministry of the Spirit that we have access through Christ to the Father (Eph. 2:18).

One of the striking features of the ministry of the Holy Spirit is that *He does not call attention to Himself.* He seeks the center stage neither in doctrine nor in an individual's experience. That belongs to Christ and the truth about Him. Consequently, to seek the Spirit for His own sake is an aberration. Many a sincere seeker after greater spiritual vitality is sadly gullible and may be led astray by Spirit-enthusiasts who are doing for the Spirit what the Spirit does not seek for Himself. The ministry of the Spirit is preeminently a functional one. He is not simply something to be admired and who in turn hopefully "turns one on." He functions to lead people to Christ so that they may know Him as Saviour and themselves as sinners. Then they may come to grips with the meaning and responsibility of discipleship and mission. This He does by teaching, guiding, comforting, helping, defending, but also by rebuking and accusing.[8]

As the Spirit comes, sent by the ascended Jesus, He comes as an inexhaustible spring, not to an elite group of Christians, but to whosoever thirsts, and believes, and obeys (John 7:37-39; 14:15, 16; Rom. 5:5). In this sense every Christian is a charismatic, and Irenaeus was right when he said, "Where the Church is, there is the Spirit, and where the Spirit of God is, there is the Church."[9]

It is a contradiction in terms and a confusion of experiences to consider oneself a Christian and yet have doubts as to whether the Spirit is present and operative in one's life. Paul said, "If a man does not possess the Spirit of Christ he is no Christian" (Rom. 8:9). It is the presence of the Spirit that enables believers today to confess with the first believers that "Jesus is Lord" (1 Cor. 12:3).

---

[1] *The Seventh-day Adventist Bible Commentary,* Ellen G. White Comments, vol. 5, p. 1078.

[2] Ellen G. White, *The Desire of Ages,* pp. 793, 805.

[3] *Ibid.,* p. 805.

[4] J. G. Dunn, *Baptism in the Holy Spirit,* p. 182.

[5] *Ibid.,* p. 187.

[6] John V. Taylor's *The Go-Between God* (London: SCM, 1972) has much sympathy for this view.

[7] Cited in M. Green, *I Believe in the Holy Spirit* (London: Hodder and Stoughton, 1975), p. 51.

[8] Ellen G. White, *Testimonies to Ministers,* p. 176.

[9] Irenaeus *Against Heresies* 3. 24. 1.

CHAPTER 4

Pentecost: The Beginning of a New Era

As previously pointed out, the Spirit, who had been present and functioning on earth since the beginning, who had come through with particular force in the person and ministry of Jesus Christ, and who had no doubt been operative in the lives of the disciples while Jesus was with them, was at the end of the three and a half years in a very special sense the gift yet to come. Several statements of Jesus, recorded by John, make that clear (John 7:39; 14:15, 16; 15:26, 27).

But this expectation of that which was "yet to come" differed from the kind of expectation every devout Jew had grown up with. For centuries the Jews had lived with the longing for the Messiah and the Spirit, whose age the Messiah would inaugurate. But fulfillment seemed remote, hidden in the mist of a very distant future. The strain placed on faith must have been considerable. "Will it ever come?" was no doubt the wistful sigh on the lips of many a devout Jew.

This, however, was not the attitude of the disciples during the days between Passover and Pentecost. Whereas their forebears had only heard the promise of the Messiah and felt a longing in their hearts, the disciples had participated in the fulfillment. Their personal experience guaranteed newness. They knew that they stood on the threshold of a completely new existence. The Messiah had come—they need look for no one else. The Messianic age had begun. The power of that age was about to be given them. There was something exciting and unparalleled about it.

The disciples who returned to Jerusalem from the Mount of Olives after the ascension of Jesus were a very different group from those dejected few who 40 days earlier had mourned the death of their Master. They could not then see beyond the grave, and their sorrow on that occasion expressed their unbelief. They could not grasp the truth that He would rise again.[1]

Now that He had ascended they returned to Jerusalem with gladness and triumph written all over their faces.[2] It was the joy of fulfillment that overflowed in their hearts—a sense of having arrived *in order to begin.* They believed that the power by which they were to be thrust into this new arena was about to break in on them. What an incredible joy to know that you are standing on the threshold of a new era—the last age, the end of which would be marked by the Lord's return! How tremendous to know that you are to play a part in spearheading the final thrust of God's kingdom! A far cry from the exercise in despair on that Saturday night 40 days earlier!

There was now no wringing of hands and asking, What shall we do next? With the commission to witness and the promise of power foremost in their thoughts, the predominant feeling no doubt was that their faith in Him had been vindicated. Their Master had made good on His promises. With this sense of trust and togetherness, the upper room was filled with an atmosphere of grace in which prayer naturally flourishes and in which spiritual cohesion among believers can be cultivated.

What did they pray about during those few days? The Bible writers do not tell us, but it would seem that Luke, who elsewhere gave a prominent place to prayer—and in connection with the gift of the Holy Spirit (for example, Luke 3:21; 11:13)—missed an opportunity here by neglecting to say that "after they had been together ten days, with one mind, in much prayer and supplication, asking for the promised Gift, the Lord heard their prayer," if that was, in fact, what they had been doing. It is significant that although they had been told to go into Jerusalem and await the gift from above, there is nothing in the record to suggest that those days constituted a prayer meeting for the gift of the Holy Spirit. The Pentecostals' appeal to this event for support that the Christian pattern manifested here is the Spirit-baptism that takes place only as a result of believers coming together to pray for the Spirit appears rather strained.

But neither was this waiting an experience in a vacuum. It was a period when they reflected on what had happened. They were saddened by their earlier unbelief and lack of understanding. In humility they confessed their sins and were comforted by the assurance of forgiveness. It was a time for strengthening the ties that bound them together as a community. It was a time for overcoming desires for self-exaltation. But above all, it was a time for commitment. They resolved to dedicate themselves totally to the task of witnessing for the resurrected and ascended Lord.[3]

The effective availability of the Spirit's power is always tied to commitment. In praying for this power in one's personal life as well as in the church, we must guard against giving the impression that we are pleading with God for a power that He is reluctant to give. The coming of this Spirit power, now as at Pentecost, depends on the condition of the receiver. If the power of the Spirit is lacking in the church today, should not the members have the courage and concern to ask the necessary questions about themselves and the spiritual community to which they belong? To sit back at such an hour and merely serve each other platitudes is surely a failure of spiritual citizenship in this last age.

The event on the day of Pentecost is described very simply in Acts 2:1-4. As they were together "suddenly there came from the sky a noise like that of a strong driving wind, which filled the whole house where they were sitting. And there appeared to them tongues like flames of fire, dispersed among them and resting on each one. And they were all filled with the Holy Spirit and began to talk in other tongues, as the Spirit gave them power of utterance."

The coming of this gift was marked by three signs: (1) the sound of "a strong driving wind"; (2) tongues like flames of fire; and (3) the gift of speaking in other tongues.

We sense our loss when we attempt to explain what these signs may actually have been. The first may well have reminded the disciples of the physical manifestation in connection with the death of Jesus (Matt. 27:51).

It is useless to try to speculate about the meaning of the tongues like flames of fire. Suffice it only to say that Pentecost was a period of a great number of physical signs, coming at the inauguration of a new era and serving purposes that the mind of the infant church was able to appreciate.

The third sign, in Acts 2:4, was that of "speaking in other tongues" (Greek: *lalein heterais glōssais*). We recognize in the last term the root of the English word "glossolalia." The fact that the word "other" is not used by Luke in his two other references to glossolalia in Acts, referring to Caesarea (Acts 10:46) and Ephesus (Acts 19:6), should not of itself be taken to imply that the tongues spoken at those places were of a different quality from those of Acts 2. We shall return to those two instances later.

Acts 2 makes it clear that there was a variety of nationalities and language groups in Jerusalem at the time. The most striking feature of the descent of the Holy Spirit on the 120 disciples was their ability to witness in a variety of languages, to the utter amazement of those who did not yet believe (verses 6ff.). Their conclusion was wrong. No, these men and women were not drunk. But the gift from above had made it possible for this band of simple and unlettered believers, who were at best only in part bilingual (Aramaic and Greek), to bring the message of what God had done in Jesus Christ to the "end of the earth."

Notice three things about this gift of the Spirit.

First, it was specifically for witnessing, that is, a movement outward from the community of faith toward those who had not heard and who did not believe, rather than an introspective movement within the community with esoteric exclusiveness.

Second, its purpose was to bring a message *from* God to humanity. The gift was not for devotional purposes or for talking with God in prayer.

Third, it had a universal element ("to all who are far away, everyone whom the Lord our God may call" [Acts 2:39]). That was the way Peter understood it when he applied the prophecy of Joel 2:28. The only conditional elements had to do with the response of individuals. When they received the gospel, repented of their sins, and expressed their decision in baptism there was nothing to prevent them from receiving the gift of the Spirit.

Who received the gift on that day? Not just the disciples, but also the 3,000. True, the passage does not say so specifically, but this conclusion is more than just a vague argument from silence if the words of Peter in Acts 2:38, 39 are to make sense. They had all repented, received forgiveness for their sins, and had been baptized. Who is to say that they were not all baptized with the Holy Spirit?

When Jesus said, "You will be baptized with the Holy Spirit and within the next few days" (Acts 1:5), fulfillment was not exhausted on the day of Pentecost. Peter testified to the openness of the promise when he said that it "is to you, and to your children, and to all who are far away" (Acts 2:39). He was no doubt aware of the witness that the Christians were to take to the Gentile world. Pentecost was the inaugural point for this wider outreach, supplemented by three subsequent experiences: at Samaria, in the house of Cornelius, and at Ephesus. We shall examine each of these briefly.

Acts 8 tells us what happened at Samaria. Philip had preached there, and a number were baptized. However, contrary to expectation (as Luke's wording in verse 16, where he used *oudepō* ["not yet"], makes clear), the gift of the Holy Spirit did not appear. He should have come in a manner obvious to both candidates and observers. One can almost sense the slight embarrassment. The searching question no doubt was "What went wrong?" The leaders at Jerusalem decided—and the record gives us no insight into their motives—to send Peter and John to look into the Samaritan situation.

Those who say that the reason for the failure of the gift to appear was that Philip had not laid his hands on the believers have completely missed the point. What was lacking was the Spirit, not an outward ritual. The only outward act required of the believers as their response in the conversion/regeneration experience was baptism, which would ensure the gift of the Spirit, as Peter said in his sermon (Acts 2:38; cf. 2:41; 8:38; 10:48; 16:15, 33; 18:8). This makes the matter all the more puzzling, for water baptism had been performed. Our answer will have to take account of two factors.

First, either there were inadequacies in Philip's teaching, or the response-in-belief of the people—although they had been baptized, something was left to be desired. The first can immediately be dismissed. Philip was subsequently called away on an evangelistic mission to an Ethiopian en route from Jerusalem to Gaza, and the record of that suggests no shortcomings on the part of Philip's teaching. But the quality of the Samaritans' response has been questioned by some. The position of Simon Magus among them even before Philip came might suggest that they were superficial, or easily swayed. If this was so, it may have colored their response to Philip.

The passage says that the people came to "believe Philip" (Acts 8:12). This wording may be significant. James G. Dunn makes an interesting, though debatable, point in his study. He says of the wording *episteusan tō Philippō* that when the verb *pisteuein* "governs a dative object (except perhaps *kurios* or *Theos*) it signifies intellectual assent to a statement or proposition, rather than commitment to God."[4]

Although the text explicitly says in verse 13 that Simon Magus himself also believed and was baptized, readers can easily infer from the rest of the story that Simon Magus never truly believed, in the Christian sense, and thus did not have the commitment that saving faith implies. Some readers, therefore, may not be able fully to escape the feeling that the Samaritans' "believing" was of a very superficial character. If that was so, it becomes obvious why they did not receive the Holy Spirit. They remained without the Spirit not because hands had not been laid on them, but because they had never really believed—a genuine faith/regeneration experience had never taken place. What this story would then teach in principle is that because the Spirit had not been received, the condition for the reception of the Spirit, namely a genuine conversion expressed in baptism, had not been met.

This argument may have much weight, but it does not fully answer the question. While superstition and religious superficiality may have been strong in that community, it is difficult to sustain the argument that the Samaritan Christians had *all* fallen short of the genuine experience.

Such failure does not come in massive communal blocks, any more than the genuine experience comes in communal blocks. There is another factor that needs to be considered.

Second, the position and authority of the apostles, as well as God's concern for safeguarding the unity of His infant church, was crucial. Fragmentation of His one holy body, the church, sad as it is at any time in history, would have been absolutely disastrous at that time. The tension between Jewish and Samaritan communities then was well known. It had a long history. For Jews, even Christians, to accept fellowship with Samaritans was very difficult. What would be more natural than for the Christian community in Jerusalem, on hearing reports of what had happened in Samaria, to ask, "Is that similar to what we have experienced?" Or, more likely, "Surely their experience was not the same as ours on the day of Pentecost. Who is to signify that they have been taught as we were?" And immediately the whole concept of an *Una Sancta* is threatened.

Rather, this is God's way of teaching the Jewish Christians, and thereby the whole church, that in Christ there are no Jews and Gentiles. Artificial distinctions are foreign to God's kingdom. The Spirit unifies. And to bring this forcefully home to the Jewish Christians, God withheld, against expectations ("not yet"), His Spirit until the apostles from Jerusalem could be there. Significantly, they were there not merely as observers to testify to the Spirit's presence, but they were instrumental in imparting the gift to those who were so hated by the Jews. In this way the Samaritan believers, by the authority vested in the apostles and accepted by the believers in Jerusalem, were brought into union with the church in Jerusalem.

Now we turn our attention to the event at Cornelius's house, recorded in Acts 10:44-48 and recounted by Peter to his brethren in Jerusalem (Acts 11:13-18). The purpose of the whole Cornelius experience, apart from the personal implication for Cornelius himself as God broke through into his life, was to teach that God's kingdom is for all people. And this was how the church in Jerusalem understood this happening ("This means that God has granted life-giving repentance to the Gentiles also" [Acts 11:18]). The similarity between Cornelius's experience and that of the disciples at Pentecost was brought out by Peter when he reached back to Pentecost and connected the two events (verses 15, 17).

The third Spirit-baptism event recorded in Acts, apart from Pentecost, is found in chapter 19, verses 1-7. It happened during Paul's ministry at Ephesus, where Apollos had just been teaching the church. The apostle found a handful of church members who were in the anomalous position of having been baptized but not having received the gift of the Spirit. Paul taught them, baptized them afresh, and laid hands on them, at which time they received the Spirit.

When Paul found them, they were not a group outside and in competition with the Christian community. They were inside the church and were described as "disciples." But the anomaly here is even more striking than at Samaria, because here at Ephesus the Spirit was not even missed. When Paul asked them about the reception of the Spirit, they confessed complete ignorance on the subject and said, in effect, "Look, we don't know what you are talking about." How incredible, since Christian baptism seems to have always been in the name of the Trinity (Matt. 28:19)!

But the matter is quickly clarified. They had been baptized with the baptism of John. When Paul met them they were no doubt committed, but he found grounds to wonder whether that commitment was in fact complete. Hence his question. We must be prepared to accept the meaning of their answer as Paul accepted it, namely, that they should be baptized in Christ's name. Rightly understood, then, the question in Acts 19:2 is not one which implies that it is possible for genuine, committed Christians not to have received the gift of the Holy Spirit (as certain Pentecostals and charismatics who view Spirit-baptism as a very valuable but still optional "extra" will argue). Instead, Paul was here asking a handful of professing believers whether they were in fact Christians!

When the dozen "disciples" confessed that they had "not even heard that there is a Holy Spirit" (19:2) significantly Paul did not give them a lecture on the Holy Spirit, followed by an intense prayer meeting in which they pleaded for that gift. He just taught them about Jesus Christ (verse 4).[5] When they accepted the truth about Him, they responded by receiving baptism in the name of Jesus, at which time they also received the Gift. The gift of the Spirit, then as now, is an inevitable consequence of genuine belief in Jesus Christ and commitment to Him. The Spirit is not the content of the gospel. That content is Christ.

The Ephesus experience clearly teaches the essential union between faith, baptism, and the gift of the Spirit.

But there are some Christians who see a lot more of a pattern-making, or normative experience, in these Spirit-events in Acts than we are prepared to accept. Specifically, some charismatics appeal to these events for support for, among other things, the following claims.

1. The baptism of the Spirit is distinctly separate from and subsequent to conversion, as is shown by both the Samaritan and the Ephesian events, but particularly by the experience of Cornelius.

2. The baptism of the Spirit is an actual event that takes place apart from the Christian baptism.

3. The book of Acts lays down a normative pattern for all Christian experience, including the laying on of hands

for the reception of the Spirit as well as the accompanying sign of speaking in tongues.

From the positions taken above, how is one to meet these assertions?

We must first of all insist that no theology can be built on certain descriptive passages in the book of Acts. These descriptions of events are brief, and one can read too much into them. The events themselves must be understood against the background of the much wider New Testament teaching. A theology must draw from the teaching of the whole Bible, and here in particular from the teachings of the New Testament. Such an approach utilizes sound hermeneutics.

Furthermore, whereas a terse description of an event may be much too inadequate to build a theology on, it may very well be adequate to communicate what Luke had in mind. Therefore, we must ask about Luke's motives in recording the events described in Acts and be prepared to confine ourselves to what the inspired mind of Luke tried to say. That is also sound hermeneutics.

Another principle we have already mentioned in our study is that one has to keep in mind the setting of events in history, and history does not stand still. Neither the tension between Jews and Samaritans in the church nor the baptism of John is with us any longer.

Luke wrote two treatises: his Gospel and Acts. The former contained "all that Jesus did and taught from the beginning" (Acts 1:1) until His ascension, and the latter "what Jesus *continued* to do after his Ascension. The second treatise might then be fittingly called 'The Acts of the Risen Christ,' or, since the Risen Christ acts through His Spirit in the Church, 'The Acts of the Holy Spirit.'"[6]

Luke's design is to show how the church responded to the commission of the risen One to take the gospel to the "ends of the earth" and to show that this was made possible through the Holy Spirit's action. He selects only those experiences that powerfully illustrate the effects of the Spirit's ministry. And what event is more fitting to begin with than Pentecost, at which time the disciples were radically changed and made into new individuals?

"The import of the event of Pentecost is that life comes to the inert, power to the impotent, enthusiasm to the bewildered, boldness to the timid."[7] Pentecost made everything—inculding themselves—look different to the disciples. They were new men. It began with Peter, whose words now show "a blending of courage, wisdom, and skill which we do not associate with him as he appears in the Gospels."[8] And it proceeded to the rest of the disciples, who were changed "from cringing cowards to fearless preachers. . . . We read of Christians making all sorts of mistakes afterwards, and they are far from being perfect. But we do not again read of them hiding away for fear of men. The Spirit altered all that."[9]

At Pentecost Peter said to his hearers that the promise of the Spirit "is to you, and to your children, and to all who are far away" (Acts 2:39). By presenting the gospel as a Spirit-movement going from Jerusalem into Judea and Samaria and to the Gentile world, Luke intended to show how this statement of Peter's was fulfilled. To do this the information he gave suffices. Surely Luke did not presume that this would serve as a foundation for a "theology of the Holy Spirit." Had that been his design he would surely have brought the considerable teaching of his associate, Paul, on this subject into his record, or at least attempted to interpret these happenings from a Pauline position. But he did nothing of the kind. Let us not demand of Luke more than he intended to say in his record.

In answering the preceding three points made by Pentecostals and neo-Pentecostals we would note several points.

1. If we were to hold, as some Pentecostals do, that Cornelius was already converted and had experienced the Christian faith-regeneration experience before Peter preached to him, we would clearly be of an opinion different from Luke's (or Peter's). Peter's preaching was specifically to "bring salvation" to Cornelius, not a post-salvation, second-stage "advanced" experience (see Acts 11:14; 15:7).

Cornelius had received much from Judaism, including a knowledge of YHWH. He was an earnest "seeker for truth,"[10] and God responded to the openness of his mind. But he could not have been born again as a result of having met Jesus Christ until the gospel of Jesus Christ had been presented to him through Peter's preaching.[11] It was while Peter preached about Jesus to the responsive centurion that the Holy Spirit descended on him. As Cornelius responded and reached out in faith, God responded by the gift of the Spirit.

The Spirit came to Cornelius, as He comes to everyone who believes, as the bearer of God's forgiveness, as the minister to communicate the reconciliation wrought in Jesus Christ. His presence in the life of Christians is not something extra. He is Himself an expression of the very forgiveness we have received and of the reconciliation that has taken place between us and God. For Cornelius, as for the disciples at Pentecost, the presence of the Spirit expressed itself in the gift of tongues. Again, this happened at the time of conversion and not at a later stage. The gift of the Spirit was *the* experience of salvation. What the experience of Cornelius bears out is that conversion (belief, repentance, and baptism by water) and baptism in the Spirit belong together, and should not be thought of as two separate events.

2. What about water-baptism and Spirit-baptism? Does the book of Acts really teach that these should be

thought of as separate experiences? No, no more than conversion and water-baptism are to be thought of as essentially separate. There is certainly nothing in the Bible to suggest that Spirit-baptism should be seen as the "encouraging cheer at the end of the first lap,"[12] or as the boisterous shouts of victory as one comes down the home stretch. Water- and Spirit-baptism, as parts of the whole conversion experience, make up the starting line, although obviously the whole process of learning, decision-making, and the public manifestation of that decision will be stretched out over a period of time, which for most will run into weeks and months.

What Acts teaches us is that the manifestation of the Spirit's presence may come immediately before water-baptism (as with Cornelius) or immediately after (as at Ephesus), but not apart from each other as though they were unrelated.

3. As for the argument that the Spirit-baptism experiences recorded in Acts are normative, or a pattern for all believers in Christ, we would again point out that neither the experience of Acts 2 nor that of Cornelius was a private, postconversion Spirit-experience of an individual believer that was to be cultivated as an aid to personal devotion. The experiences were church-*founding* phenomena, and they had a distinct corporate nature. There was something inaugural about them to mark the beginning of the era of the ascended Lord and of the church's witness to Him.

While there is no doubt that the experience of the Spirit on the day of Pentecost, manifested in the speaking of tongues, was a means to help the disciples overcome language barriers, these phenomena were clearly inaugural signs. They told the disciples that the period of waiting was over and that the time of the church's mission had come. They told Cornelius and the believers in Samaria that God was authenticating what had happened in their communities in the name of Christ. In these ways God was saying that all those who had faith in Jesus Christ were children of Abraham and heirs according to the promise. And, in view of the Jewish tradition on that point, no less than an emphatic statement would do.

By mighty signs and wonders God said to that early community of believers that a new era with new opportunities in the ascended Lord had come. Through them He showed that He was prepared to give the believers, committed to witnessing, unlimited power to enter the kingdom.

---

[1] Ellen G. White, *The Acts of the Apostles* (Mountain View, Calif.: Pacific Press Pub. Assn.), p. 26.

[2] *Ibid.,* p. 35.

[3] *Ibid.,* pp. 36, 37; *Christ's Object Lessons* (Washington, D.C.: Review and Herald Pub. Assn.), p. 327.

[4] J. G. Dunn, *Baptism in the Holy Spirit,* p. 65.

[5] White, *The Acts of the Apostles,* pp. 282, 283.

[6] F. F. Bruce, *The Acts of the Apostles* (Grand Rapids: Wm. B. Eerdmans, 1953), p. 30.

[7] J. C. Haughey, *The Conspiracy of God: The Holy Spirit in Men,* p. 82.

[8] H. B. Swete, *The Holy Spirit in the New Testament* (Grand Rapids: Baker Book House), p. 76.

[9] L. Morris, *Spirit of the Living God* (London: InterVarsity Press, 1974), p. 53.

[10] White, *The Acts of the Apostles,* pp. 131ff.

[11] *Ibid.,* p. 136.

[12] P. Crowe, "Sacraments and Mission," *Evangelical Essays on Church and Sacraments,* ed. C. Buchanan (London: SPCK, 1972), p. 35.

CHAPTER 5

The Gift and the Gifts of the Spirit

Baptism in or of the Holy Spirit is the gift of the Spirit Himself. The bestowal of this gift has two phases: one in history and the other in an individual's experience. Just as Jesus came at one point in history, but nevertheless does not become my Lord until I am drawn by Him and respond by accepting Him, so the Spirit, who came to the community of believers at Pentecost as a gift to the church (and that gift has never been withdrawn), must find access to my life in order for the gift to become real *to me*. How does that happen?

Some charismatics and Pentecostals, in quest of an updated version of Wesley's "second blessing," will have us believe that it is possible to be baptized separately into each person of the Trinity. We are told that having been baptized by water into Christ at conversion, albeit by the ministry of the Spirit, we must now, by the ministry of Christ, press on to baptism into the Spirit. The first blessing is the experience of faith; the second, of power. Is that what the Bible teaches?

Look again at Paul's experience at Ephesus. He asked the 12 men specifically, "What baptism were you given?" (Acts 19:3). On learning that it was the baptism of John, he taught them about Jesus Christ. When they were brought to the point of believing in Him, they received the Gift. Frederick Dale Bruner, in his interesting study of this subject,[1] mentions three questions that Paul could have asked the dozen men at Ephesus had the above Pentecostal claim been valid.

1. "Did you not know that after mere faith you are to press on to a second experience where you will receive an endowment of power through the baptism in the Holy Spirit?"

2. "Who then laid hands on you?" or "Did you fail to visit (or call) the apostles?"

3. "Did you fail to believe *enough?*"

However, all these questions were irrelevant. The only thing that mattered was the position of Jesus Christ in their lives. It was in *that* respect that something was lacking.

We ask the question How does the Gift already bestowed on the church become our Gift? The simple answer that comes from the Ephesus experience (verses 1-6) is that it becomes ours when we receive the resurrected Lord—not as a means to a further end (for instance, the Holy Spirit), but as *the end* to all our needs and longings.

What a sad state of affairs (is it not also an exercise in idolatry?) when a community of believers divides itself into the Spirit-filled ones and the rank and file of the church, who have no access to the same power! Such a situation distorts biblical truth, and the distinction collapses by virtue of the Bible's definition of what a Christian is (Rom. 8:9). The fact that one is a child of God means that one is truly led by the Spirit of God (verse 14).

John, taking up the same thought, writes: "This is [God's] command: to give our allegiance to his Son Jesus Christ and love one another." When we do that "he dwells in us. And this is how we can make sure that he dwells within us: we know it from the Spirit he has given us" (1 John 3:23, 24). Further, "Here is the proof that we dwell in him and he dwells in us: he has imparted his Spirit to us" (1 John 4:13).

And did not Paul, in writing to the believers in one church, make the point that "your body is a shrine of the indwelling Holy Spirit, and the Spirit is God's gift to you" (1 Cor. 6:19)?

The whole idea of "Jesus Christ plus," whether it be in regard to rituals and ceremonies, deeds of the law, or a separable Spirit-phenomenon, is in the context of our discussion a perversion of the biblical doctrine of salvation. It pleased the Father, in the words of Paul, that in Christ the fullness of the Godhead should dwell bodily (Col. 2:9).

Recognizing one's membership in the community is invaluable to the unity of the church. Elitism leads to fragmentation. Paul comes again to our help in 1 Corinthians 12:13, where he makes his point in the context of baptism. All who have accepted Jesus Christ are by baptism brought "into one body." This body is, of course, that of Christ, which is the church. The one thing that those who are thus incorporated in Christ have in common is that "one Holy Spirit was poured out for all of us to drink." The hallmark of genuine Christians—and if we are not genuine, we are hardly Christians—is that we have "had a taste of the heavenly gift and a share in the Holy Spirit" (Heb. 6:4). Here lies our commonness.[2]

But this our one common gift, the Spirit, shows Himself enormously resourceful in His choice of ways and means to surface and function within the community of believers. Here lies our diversity.

How many different gifts of the Spirit are there? By the activities of certain contemporary Spirit-enthusiasts, one would think that there were only three: tongues, healing, and prophecy—graded in that order. Both the list and the grading are wrong. We find in the New Testament four separate lists of spiritual gifts, and the contexts in which they are placed give us some idea of their functions. The passages are 1 Corinthians 12:4-7; Ephesians 4:8-12; Romans 12:3-8; and 1 Peter 4:10, 11.

One student compared these lists and concluded that there are at least 20 distinct gifts referred to. In fact, the differences between the lists are greater than their similarities. Furthermore, the investigation revealed that no single gift occurs in all lists. Finally, 13 of the gifts are mentioned only once.[3] To add up the number of gifts enumerated in order to establish how many possible varieties of spiritual gifts there may be is to completely miss the point of the lists.

It is impossible for us to define the exact nature of all of these gifts listed by Paul and Peter. For instance, can we accurately distinguish between the "oracles of God" (1 Peter 4:11, KJV); "word of wisdom" (1 Cor. 12:8, KJV); and "exhortation" (Rom. 12:8, KJV)? And if there is a difference, can we then distinguish these shades from "prophecy," which three of the lists specifically mention? No doubt the believers in the primitive church knew what the writers had in mind, but a simple translation of the words leaves us still asking questions.

The New English Bible has tried to come to our aid by giving us an interpreted list rather than a translation of the Greek. For example, the translators consistently and incorrectly translate the 17 occurrences of *glōssa* in 1 Corinthians 12-14 as "ecstatic utterance" or "tongues of ecstasy," which does not at all help us understand what these gifts stood for in the lives of those early believers. To identify one of the *charismata* in these lists with a real or so-called spiritual manifestation of our own days is to take for granted an identity that is yet to be established.

Let us take note of what Paul says in the opening verses of 1 Corinthians 12.

1. The members of the community who needed the

corrective message that Paul was about to give were marked by traits of instability and gullibility. They all were too easily swept off their feet. Paul says to them, "That is what you were really like when I first met you" (see verse 2). But although they had now shifted their loyalty from their pagan gods to Jesus Christ, it would seem that, sadly, their basic instability had not changed. Paul had already rebuked them for their spiritual immaturity (1 Cor. 3:1ff.). So he says that their misguided quest for spirituality (particularly reflected in chapter 14) was really nothing but a further evidence of their weak character and spiritual immaturity.

2. Only those who are seriously prepared to confess the lordship of Jesus Christ are led by the Holy Spirit (1 Cor. 12:3)! This was no mere utterance of words. Every age, also that of Corinth, has had its own countercry "Caesar is Lord," which is to say "Accursed is Jesus." Our basic loyalties are at stake. To confess that "Jesus is Lord" (cf. Phil. 2:11) means to live a life of doxology, at the center of which is Jesus Christ. "How do you, Corinthians, reconcile your 'ego-enthralling'[4] search for the spectacular with the confession 'Jesus is Lord'?" Paul asks.

Again, the question of Spirit-filledness is identical with the question of the place and position of Jesus Christ in one's life. The Holy Spirit exalts only One as the Lord. Now, as in the days of the early church, the "Spirit is constantly at work, seeking to draw the attention of men to the great sacrifice made on the cross of Calvary."[5] You can be sure that a church member who is involved in some subtle exercise of "self-deification" lacks the Holy Spirit. Spirit-filledness is identical with Christ being all in all, which is to confess that "Jesus is Lord."[6]

3. Not only do the gifts *(charismata)* vary greatly, but, says Paul, so do services *(diakoniai)* and works *(energēmata)* (1 Cor. 12:4-6). An interesting set of triplets! Apparently, Paul wanted to remind the misguided Corinthian enthusi-

asts that although they may have had a "swept-off-the-feet" preoccupation with one particular *charismata,* namely tongues, there was a vast variety not only of *charismata* but also of diakoniai and *energēmata* with which to confess that "Jesus is Lord."

The "services" and "works" are, as such, not really separate and different from the "gifts." They are the possibilities and situations in which the gifts function. Together they are spiritual capacities with real-life opportunities. John Stott describes them as "a gift and the job in which to exercise it, or a job and the gift with which to do it."[7]

4. These gifts are all given "for some useful purpose" (verse 7; "for the common good," RSV). The connected thought of service should make it clear that Paul is not writing about an endowment "for the private enjoyment of self-cultivation of the individual, but [about] a spiritual responsibility . . . given to be exercised for the edification of others."[8]

So Paul here turns his back decisively on any view that treasures gifts for their value to the receiver. The question for Paul is Of what value is it to the church? No wonder, then, that the apostle decided that were the Corinthians to overcome their overenthusiasm they would need to understand (a) what it meant to be part of a larger community—the church—and (b) what it meant to be guided by love. So before Paul returns to the misguidedness of the Corinthians in chapter 14, he dwells with beautiful simplicity on these two themes.

As Spirit and gifts express unity and diversity, so Paul presents unity in diversity by using the idea of the body as an expression of the church. In the church a great variety of gifts of the Spirit will be exercised by many different people (1 Cor. 12:14-26). But although the limbs and organs of the body act differently, they are nevertheless expressions of an inner unity of purpose and work in the interest of that unity.

The gifts of the Spirit are to function with coordination in the interest of the church and its unity.[9] Spiritual quirks are not only distracting, but they must be tempered in the interest of the common good lest they become obsessions. These are, of course, counterproductive to the workings of the Spirit and the function of the church. This is where the Corinthian community fell down.

Furthermore, in the midst of the exercise of spiritual gifts in Corinth, feelings of inferiority and superiority, related to the display of the more spectacular gift of tongues, abounded. By a very open exaltation of that particular gift, suggesting subtly at least that those who did not have the gift were still in the "amateur league," the church in that city was divided into the spiritual haves and have-nots. As a result, people were looking with suspicion and envy at one another, but not able to love. And this will be the case in every community in which such an attitude is displayed.

In dealing with that side of the problem, "Paul speaks to all of us who spend most of our time either wishing that we were someone else, or glad that we aren't."[10] His answer is simple: We need each other; let us not burn ourselves out in envy, suspicion, and feelings of superiority. Every gift of the Spirit is honorable, and everyone can contribute something to the growth of the body. Without this variety the growth is stunted.

So who looks down upon whom in my spiritual community? Shall the theologian, who, with his professional training, has a sharper ability to read the "fine print," look down upon his fellow worker, "Brother Evangelist," who, in his opinion, is equipped to appreciate the "fat headlines" only? Or shall the evangelist on the front lines, proclaiming God's truth, look down upon the theologian, who, in his opinion, lives in an ivory tower out of touch with the real world and with no appreciation of the real questions that people "out there" ask?

This tension between "cerebral" and "practical" Christianity is not just the reserve of the professionals. It surfaces in many a church where some who have found a "real" Christian experience regard others as nonstarters with "just a lot of theory." Conversely, those who find richness in taxing their minds to a maximum understanding of truth and biblical concepts regard those who cannot follow them on this course as simpletons guided by sheer emotion.

Most of us easily forget that in the New Testament lists of spiritual gifts there is great variety. But the various gifts the New Testament describes are for sharing with and receiving from others. Those who refuse to receive from another's spiritual experience have no one with whom to share their own experiences. That inevitably spells spiritual death. We cannot survive as loners! We need each other because we are "bonded and knit together," and the body of the church grows only "through the due activity of each part" (Eph. 4:16). One writer forcefully stated: "The Spirit animates a Body, not monads. Each new cell or dead cell comes to life through the touch of other members of the Body of Christ who are animated by the Spirit. The loner who claims he is being led by the Spirit is a liar."[11]

So, what causes this tension, envy, suspicion, these feelings of inferiority or superiority? The cause, says Paul, is lack of love. For that reason the thirteenth chapter of 1 Corinthians is no incidental, parenthetical insertion between chapters 12 and 14. It was the heart of the whole matter. Lack of love was the root of the Corinthian abuse of the gifts. Lack of love will always destroy the usefulness of any gift of the Spirit, however exalted it may be.

Apropos of exalted gifts, the conclusions that the Corinthians drew about the meaning and value of their gifts were wrong. That is another reason for our earlier objection to the list of "tongues, healing, and prophecy—graded in that order." All spiritual gifts have functional purposes. To suppress a gift and deny its function means to lose it. When the Spirit comes His presence is discernible, and in the lives of some individuals at certain times in history He is seen more miraculously than in others. The particular gift an individual receives is, however, not the basis for measuring the quality of that believer's spiritual experience. By exalting tongues as the quintessence of spirituality, the Corinthians made a mistake as, on the whole, Pentecostal and charismatic communities do today. To grade a community's spiritual experience along these lines is to get trapped in the "attractive" (if your gift is one of the three) circuit of self-exaltation. To do this is also to live in the sin of idolatry.

Rather, if it is really the Holy Spirit who has entered your life, the first thing He will do is to "burn away the dross of selfishness, and reveal a love which is tried in fire, a love that maketh rich."[12] Assessing others' spiritual experience not only is a perverse pastime but also is profoundly nonspiritual and, in the end, self-destructive.

Put simply, then, the force of Paul's point to the Corinthian believers is that if love is not being revealed, the gifts being exercised go against the very design of the Holy Spirit and, at least implicitly, should lead to the question of whether they are in fact of the Spirit, and not self-generated. The hallmark of love is that it does not seek its own; it is more willing to forgo its rights than to claim and assert them.

Apart from the general message that the gifts of the Spirit are essential for the spiritual progress of the church, Paul makes two points as crucial for the church today as for then.

1. Spiritual gifts are given to individuals *as members of the body of Christ.* Those who receive such a gift must recognize that the scope for private "enjoyment" is at least very limited. The whole tenor of Paul's argument to the "enthusi-

asts" at Corinth—and this comes through in more places than 1 Corinthians 12-14—was that community interests take precedence over private religious preoccupations. The gifts were given in the main to build up the church. In chapter 14 Paul refers to the "building up" of the church no less than five times, and Peter's advice to his community of believers was: "Whatever gift each of you may have received, use it in service to one another" (1 Peter 4:10). This is the fellowship *(koinōnia)* of the Spirit. But these gifts are also to some extent connected with the mission of the church. The church is commissioned to evangelize the world. That is the primary purpose for which it exists. Therefore, spiritual endowments are made to equip and facilitate a missionary movement (see Eph. 4:12).

2. A corollary of this is that the gifts are to be exercised in conjunction with, not apart from, the church, which is the body of Christ. If they are pursued in defiance of the needs of that body, they discredit themselves. If they are not governed by the love of which Paul spoke in chapter 13, their loud and noisy exercises—and those characteristics are not exclusive with tongues—are the self-disclosures of perversions and aberrations.

Here lies the acid test of spiritual gifts.

In grading the gifts, why should the teaching gifts be at the top in the New Testament? Is it not because of their great importance in building up a community? Because building up and equipping for service is the main purpose of the gifts, it is not at all strange that the teaching ministry should feature so prominently on all four lists of gifts mentioned earlier. Whether it be given to apostles or prophets, or whether it be the gift of wise speech, or speaking the oracles of God, it is the teaching ministry.

It is when the mind lies fallow that it is vulnerable. Then it begins to seek substitutes for the knowledge and understanding of truth, finding what is no doubt a deeply felt satisfaction in contacts with spectaculars that seem to have the stamp of the supernatural on them. But this satisfaction is artificial and deceptive. Such an encounter is in some respects akin to that other intruder into Christian experience that Paul would call "deeds of the law," namely, that circuit of activities in which one misguidedly becomes involved to merit salvation or demonstrate worthiness of it. Not only are both of these unwholesome cravings for the tangible, but also both can accept as real only what one can touch, feel, hear, see, or smell. Both are failures of faith, and in the end both will fail one. And believers must confess again that God is to be found neither in the "mighty wind" nor in the "earthquake." For their own sake this is a discovery they need to make before the end of the day.

Though in the thoughts of Paul particularly our spiritual corporateness—our belonging to a body—is given such strong emphasis, Paul never allows this emphasis to eclipse individuality. Ephesians 4:16 and Colossians 2:19 make it clear that though the various "joints and ligaments" function in the interest of the whole body, they don't all do the same job. This is where so many of us stumble when we see the church more as an organization than as an organism and look at our individual functions more as "offices" than as services. Consequently, some feel insecure or threatened, and anti-individuality, anti-spontaneity, anti-laity defense mechanisms are put into motion. Even in a highly programmed Christianity we must tirelessly work to overcome our suspicion of one another. We must learn to discover afresh the love that Paul unfolded to the Corinthians and which is found in trust, recognition of interdependence, and acceptance of one another as genuine, without waiting for the proofs to be weighed and tested.

At this point in our discussion, we must deal with an important and sensitive point. It has to do with feelings and felt needs in one's worship life. Though one may, on reflection, agree with the Roman Catholic abbot who, writing of the spiritual life, observed that feelings are "useful for the beginners . . . but not to be depended on,"[13] many Christians are either beginners or have not learned that feelings are "not to be depended on." In their spiritual lives feelings matter enormously. They need a continuous and conscious sense of God's presence in their own personal experience and hunger for a greater involvement in their community's acts of worship.

A church whose act of worship is liturgical gives the people a feeling of dryness, being lifeless, and, although participating, they do not *feel* that they have really entered into true worship. There is so much receiving, they say, but little opportunity for response. Every church that, in its public acts of worship, limits its participants' possibilities of response to the singing of two or three hymns and the giving of offerings needs to ask itself whether or not some liturgical loosening up could be made. How can I as a minister make the celebration of the sacraments, particularly the Communion, become an occasion when the individual believer's need for involvement and response can better be met? Although I must guard the doctrines as being of the Lord and rooted in the teachings of the apostles, our liturgy or order of church services need not be similarly protected.

Some will say that feelings and faith must not be confused. That's difficult to argue with. Yet, on reflection, it may be difficult to make such a neat and clean division between the two. After all, faith is an experience—an experience of responding to the revelation of God, which is an experience of the whole person. As our gifts are different, so are our needs, and at times also our ways of responding to God. We should all beware of what one writer calls "programmatic spirituality,"[14] in which responses in worship, adequate and genuine for some, are for others only an act of going through the motions. If that is what they are, then that which for some is a means to facilitate worship and communion with God is for others a barrier against it.

Returning to the subject of gifts of the Spirit: What is the relationship between such gifts and natural talents? Some will say they are identical, and in that way they *naturally* account for spiritual gifts. We cannot share that view. True, the two may often overlap. And in bestowing a particular gift on an individual, God may well make His choice with a view to the individual's natural talents. But even as one makes that observation, examples come to mind of the unlikeliest of individuals on whom God has chosen to bestow a gift of the Spirit. (Ellen G. White appears in this tradition.) Their availability, together with their uncompromising devotion to God and His church, is what must have counted.[15]

We do not have to look far to find people who are talented or personally gifted—the combined contributions of heredity, education, and discipline. But these talents, often exercised in activities that can hardly be associated with God's kingdom, cannot be described as gifts of the Spirit. Gifts of the Spirit are especially bestowed on God's people for their upbuilding and for equipping the church for its mission. When, however, we surrender self to God, we surrender our talents as well. God then returns to us our talents "purified and ennobled, to be used for His glory in blessing our fellow men."[16]

Here is where it is impossible to draw a distinct line between talents and some spiritual gifts, since if the gifts are not identical with the talents in these instances they at least function through them. What we are saying is that some spiritual gifts dovetail with the natural talents of individuals committed to Christ.

But that can be so only with some gifts. Others (for example, prophecy and healing) defy natural talents, education, and discipline. They are not improved by use. They are not barometers of any particularly advanced kind of spirituality. Without attempting to explore God's mind, we can say only that they are gifts bestowed by a God who sees the needs of the church, the availability of His servants, and their individual humility and devotion. But God is sovereign, and His decision is free.

But what about 1 Corinthians 13:8, 9, which says: "Are there prophets? their work will be over. Are there tongues of ecstasy? they will cease. Is there knowledge? it will vanish away"? Some Christians conclude from Paul's words that the gifts of the Spirit are not for today. They have died out. They must, they say, be regarded as gifts "for the time of the church's infancy. They did not last for very long, and in the providence of God evidently they were not expected to last for very long."[17] These gifts, it is argued, all served just to inaugurate the Christian dispensation and were then withdrawn. What is one to say to this?

We earlier took the position that simply because a phenomenon of the Spirit occurred in the early church is in itself no basis for asserting that it is normative for all subsequent Christian experience. The times and the needs are not the same. We took that position particularly with regard to manifestations of tongues and explained our reasoning then.

But such a line of reasoning is very different from saying that God has withdrawn the spiritual gifts that the early church knew. Were we to say that, we would have to follow the assertion with the further claim that God has also abandoned His whole scheme of selecting a spiritual community to spearhead the activities of His kingdom in a fallen world. It is inconceivable that such a community could exist unless God supplied its needs. Not only is such a position completely unnecessary, but there is no hint in the Bible of such a withdrawal.

One suspects that many who have taken the position that the gifts have been withdrawn have formulated their position in order to answer charismatics and Pentecostals.[18] But surely their answer reflects some of the imbalance of an overreaction. Take, as an example, the gift of healing.

Charismatics often say that God wants people never to be ill. He wills all to be healed, and "we have no scriptural warrant to end a healing prayer with the faith-destroying phrase 'If it be Thy will'!"[19]

Michael Green wrote a good answer to that.[20] He said that "one does not get the impression that [healing] played a major part in the spread of the gospel in early times." Supporting evidence includes the indication that although both Peter and Paul exercised the gift of healing in Acts, they were not always able to heal and had to leave friends ill without apparently being able to do anything about it (2 Tim. 4:20; Phil. 2:25-27) and that God, on occasion, instead of healing gives strength to bear one's suffering (2 Cor. 12:7-9).

Furthermore, in a world plagued with sin, why should we as Christians think that we have a right to be free from the pains of the present world? "Suffering, sin, disease and death are all part of the fallen lot of mankind, and they will be with us until heaven."[21] And, as Green observes correctly: "How people would rush to Christianity (and for all the wrong motives) if it carried with it automatic exemption from sickness! What a nonsense it would make of Christian virtues like longsuffering, patience, and endurance."

No, the charismatics' position is wrong, as ours would be were we to opt for the other extreme, which holds that the gift of healing has been withdrawn. God heals today as in the days of the early believers, but His choice of means may differ with time and place. He can work today through the sharp tools of medical science. In another age, or even today in parts of the world where the benefits of medical science are very limited, God has stepped in and performed His healing ministry, as He wills, in more spectacular ways, as numerous examples from ages past and from the developing world today show. Even in our environment of advanced medical science, God has shown that He is not limited by that science and has outpaced it with the touch of His healing hand. As the gift of the Spirit is permanent so is the Spirit's bestowal of gifts. But the God who acts does so in response to needs, and they are not fixed for all times, places, and peoples.

In these answers we have responded also to that other kind of "dispensationalist" who suggests that Christianity is presently in a spiritual drought that will pass; that spiritual gifts are not presently with us, but that we shall see a revival of them in the future. This kind of thinking to justify our own spiritual decay is without the least shred of biblical support.[22] God is alive and well. He is acting in His church and for His people now as He has in the past. And He will continue to do so as long as we are here. Failure in this area lies with us and not with God.

---

[1] F. D. Bruner, *A Theology of the Holy Spirit* (Grand Rapids: William B. Eerdmans, 1970), pp. 209, 210.

[2] See Ellen G. White, *Testimonies for the Church* (Mountain View, Calif.: Pacific Press Pub. Assn., 1948), vol. 1, p. 159.

[3] John R. W. Stott, Baptism and Fullness: *The Work of the Holy Spirit* (London: InterVarsity Press, 1975), p. 88.

[4] Bruner, p. 287.

[5] Ellen G. White, *Gospel Workers,* p. 286.

[6] *Ibid.,* p. 287; Testimonies, vol. 1, p. 303.

[7] Stott, p. 87.

[8] J. Goldingay, *The Church and the Gifts of the Spirit* (Bramcote, Notts: Grove Books, 1972), p. 6.

[9] Ellen G. White, *Testimonies to Ministers,* p. 29.

[10] Goldingay, p. 9.

[11] J. C. Haughey, *The Conspiracy of God: The Holy Spirit in Men,* p. 94.

[12] White, *Testimonies to Ministers,* p. 154.

[13] *The Spiritual Letters of Dom John Chapman* (London: Sheed & Ward, 1946), p. 99.

[14] Haughey, p. 98f.

[15] Ellen G. White, *Christ's Object Lessons,* p. 328.

[16] *Ibid.*

[17] L. Morris, *Spirit of the Living God,* pp. 63, 64.

[18] The book by Dennis and Rita Bennett, *The Holy Spirit and You* (London: Coverdale, 1971), is a clear expression of how charismatics understand the gifts of the Spirit.

[19] Bennett, *ibid.,* p. 114.

[20] M. Green, *I Believe in the Spirit,* pp. 175, 176.

[21] *Ibid.*

[22] White, *Testimonies to Ministers,* pp. 174, 175.

CHAPTER 6

The Spirit's Points of Entry

While I was sitting in a small Bible study circle in which we were sharing thoughts on the Spirit's real presence, a young student asked with sincerity and concern, "How can I be really *sure* that the Holy Spirit is present with me?"

Another tried to answer this with a further question: "Well, how can you be really sure that you're a Christian? I mean, how do you *know* that you've really given yourself to Jesus Christ?"

Slowly and with reflection the first student said, "Yes, I see what you mean."

Yet somehow I suspect that that was exactly what she did not see.

That student's difficulty was like that of so many sincere Christians: If God has really given me this great gift, why is my Christian experience at this moment in such a mess? Where is my joy? What has happened to the hopes I had, to say nothing of the victories I longed for? How am I to identify the Spirit in my life, or can the Spirit be isolated and identified by Himself?

I fear that we are plaguing ourselves by creating our own uncertainties.

Let us see how the Bible presents the Spirit's points of entry into our lives. We shall also examine what He does *to* us and *for* us. At the end of this chapter I hope that we shall have a clearer picture of the assertion we have already made several times, namely, that to be a genuine Christian and to lead a committed life is in fact to confess to the real presence of the Holy Spirit.

1. Our starting place is a well-known statement of Jesus: "But when your Advocate has come . . . he will bear witness to me" (John 15:26). Note also these words of His about the Holy Spirit: "He will glorify me, for everything that he makes known to you he will draw from what is mine" (John 16:14). The Gift becomes the Giver. He is the one who makes Jesus Christ come alive to us. He is not an alternative revelation. He is the Spirit of truth, yes, but He is not an alternative truth to that brought and taught by Him who says that He is the truth (John 14:6), "for everything that he makes known to you he will draw from what is mine" (John 16:14).

Jesus Christ is not just an idea or an enigmatic point of reference in some religio-political ideology. He is not a recurring figure who comes afresh in each new "liberation" struggle. He walked about on earth some 2,000 years ago. He taught some very specific things. He lived a life in which His actions spoke as loudly as His sayings. And He is unique. The Spirit brings to us all that Jesus Christ stood for when He was "in the flesh."

But this Jesus who walked the shores of Galilee steps out of the past and into our lives as He comes to us from *the Gospels.* We have no other way of knowing Him, and the Spirit is not an alternative to the Gospels to show us Christ. In this sense, therefore, it is inconceivable that the Spirit will communicate Jesus Christ to diligent, prayerful searchers of Scripture in a way that will cause them to say, "Is that You, Lord? Oh! I just didn't recognize You!"

While the Holy Spirit will always lead us to confess our inadequate understanding of Christ, and in that sense cause the freshness of daybreak to come our way continuously, there is a clear continuity and identity between the Lord seen in the Gospels and the One communicated by the Spirit. And the committed mind will recognize Him.

2. Rather than leading me to ask, "Is that You, Lord?" the Spirit, as He communicates the living Lord, is more likely to lead me to ask, "Lord, is this really me? Is this the way I really am?" My grief at being so appallingly different from Him breaks through. I recognize how I have let Him down, how I have sought my own interests instead of His, and I feel undone. Again I am reminded of those words from *Steps to Christ,* page 64: "The closer you come to Jesus, the more faulty you will appear in your own eyes."

This phase of the Spirit's ministry is what we generally call conviction of sin. In the same breath in which Jesus said that the Spirit would communicate Him, He said that the Spirit's ministry would also consist of showing the world "where wrong and right and judgement lie. He will convict them of wrong" (John 16:8, 9). This comes in our individual experience when we see ourselves in contrast to Christ. It is the contrast that is so striking. Sin is always against the person of our Lord, rather than being the violation of certain detached or abstract points.

3. We mentioned the grief that overcomes us. This is the work of the Spirit, who leads us to the point of repentance. We may well have been successful in fooling "some of the people [including ourselves] some of the time," but a genuinely repentant person stops pretending. Efforts to rationalize and justify become totally useless. The spiritual mirror is there, and the Spirit gives me grace to lift my eyes and focus my sight. What I see makes me join voices with those who have similarly seen and cried out, "Friends, what are we to do?" (Acts 2:37).

We see both what we are and what we could become, and the contrast is not a beautiful one. A deeply intense but perhaps barely perceived "Help me!" arises from our distressed hearts, followed by a determined "I've got to get out of this! No matter what the results, I've got to stop this drift into self-destruction!"

This experience of repentance contains the divine-human mixture of despair and hope—and praise be to God for both! Repentance means the turning away of the whole person from one orientation or direction to another. It means the radical renouncing of one way of living and the embarking upon a totally new way—the way of the risen Lord. "Repent" has always been the first call God makes to His people. That was the message of the prophets of old. Similarly, in the New Testament, whether in the preaching of John the Baptist or in the later Christian proclamation, the call to repentance stood first (Matt. 3:2; 4:17; Acts 2:38).

We would fail were we to try to differentiate between conviction and repentance for, as in so many other stages of our Christian experience, we cannot separate one from the other. It is only for the convenience of study that we can look at them individually.

The greatest sin of all is the sin of idolatry. It is also the most common one. To repent means first of all to turn away from our preoccupation with ourselves and make God the center of our lives. And if it is repentance, and the Spirit is in it, it will affect the whole life. God never settles for a substitute, be it a double tithe, the consecration of some talent, or the giving of some hours per week to fill an office in the church.

Repentance as an act of renouncing our idols, of turning away from our preoccupation with ourselves to God, is something that keeps occurring throughout the Christian life. It is our constant renewal, and only death—spiritual or otherwise—will bring an end to the experience of repentance.

It is the ministry of the Spirit to make us aware of the futility of worshiping our idols, to make us see the lengths to which we will go to find substitutes for the Lord Jesus Christ, and to cause us to mourn at the ways in which we have let Him down. But it is also the ministry of the Spirit to make us see, during these moments of despair, the real hope that God offers. The Spirit is not in the business of creating despair for despair's sake (what a morbid condition that would be were we to remain at this point!) but for the sake of leading us to reconciliation, to finding a life of hope, joy, and the peace that is "beyond our utmost understanding" (Phil. 4:7; cf. Rom. 8:6; 15:13; 1 Peter 5:14).

4. The next moment of the Spirit's ministry is in giving assurance. He begins this by reminding believers that the course they have embarked on is not an uncertain one laid out on one's own initiative. The Spirit reminds us of the words of the departing Jesus to His disciples, "You did not choose me: I chose you. I appointed you to go on and bear fruit, . . . so that the Father may give you all that you ask in my name" (John 15:16).

The assurance that it is God who is the mover behind our newly chosen direction is important to insist on. Unsettling questions about whether we might not be victims of circumstances, enthusiasm, or even delusions could not otherwise satisfactorily be resolved. This despite the fact that Calvin and those who are similarly convinced bring to us distortions of the divine initiative in a doctrine of predestination. But what they are doing is to present us with "a God not worthy to be worshiped," in the words of John Macquarrie. A religious experience is one in which God acts for, through, and in a human being. It would be very inadequate to view such an experience primarily as an act of the individual. Needless to say, this is not an experience in which, as one writer would have us believe, "man is 100 percent passive, and the Holy Spirit

100 percent active." *No* kind of dynamic relationship, not to mention love, could begin to grow in that kind of setting. Relationships such as we are speaking of demand a constant interchange between stimulus and response, between God and humanity.

Let us go back to the questions How do I know the Spirit's presence is with me? How can I be sure?

It is right for us to seek certainty. God wants His children to feel secure and assured. He wants them to have the same certainty as Paul did ("For I am convinced . . ."; "I know who it is in whom I have trusted, and am confident of his power"; "Let us be firm and unswerving in the confession of our hope, for the Giver of the promise may be trusted" [Rom. 8:38; 2 Tim. 1:12; Heb. 10:23]). Such a frame of mind is absolutely vital in order to survive as believers during times of doubt, agnosticism, and secularism. The invitation to "come boldly unto the throne of grace" (Heb. 4:16, KJV) demands a very basic conviction.

The Spirit is meant to give us certainty, and 1 John should help us find answers to the questions we raised. John wrote that letter specifically to assure the believers of eternal life (1 John 5:13). He said: "When we keep his commands we dwell in him and he dwells in us. And this is how we can make sure that he dwells within us: we know it from the Spirit he has given us" (1 John 3:24).

As to the grounds for this spiritual certainty, we shall have to recognize that there are two extremes, both of which fall short of the truth. On the one hand, spiritual certainty is not a vague, mystical "Spirit-in-me-ism" that confirms the experience to my spirit in a way that defies all understanding and reason. Were it such, we would be left wide open to all the charges of self-deception. But it is an inner assurance that is more than the sum of my knowledge and understanding. My whole being, including my emotions, is affected by it. There comes to me a real sense of belonging that I find myself unable to capture with words, arguments, or bits of information. But I know it is real! This was no doubt in Paul's mind when he wrote that the "Spirit of God joins with our spirit in testifying that we are God's children" (Rom. 8:16).

This certainty may well be more than my knowledge and understanding, but it does not defy understanding. It may be an inner assurance, yes, but it does not originate solely from within. It grows in a mysterious and imperceptible way out of reading, reflecting, praying, and living a responsive and committed life. In other words, the assurance of which we are speaking comes out of a complete life with God, and its hallmark is humility. In any case, it is difficult to see how a Christian can witness with any kind of conviction without such assurance (1 Thess. 1:5).

But John points to some specific evidence that should serve to give confidence to believers, or that at least exposes and condemns false security. He puts the question to believers: What has happened to your life? Is it changed? The Spirit's presence should make a difference. John is very firm on this. In the life of all believers there must be a sense of obedience "to his word" (1 John 2:5). "The test [is] . . . to live as Christ himself lived" (verse 6). Obviously we cannot go on cultivating the same way of life as we did when we were part of the world (1 John 3:9, 13, 14). This does not mean that the pull of the world is gone; it means only that one has chosen to move in a different direction.

In his study on the Holy Spirit Michael Green puts it very well: "Of course John does not mean that the Christian becomes sinless overnight. He knows full well that Christians can and do sin, and if we pretend otherwise we are lying (1:8, 10). But he is insisting, in black and white terms, that the divine sonship, mediated by the Spirit, must show itself in changed behavior. We cannot go on untouched in the old self-centered ways if the Holy Spirit has made his residence within us."[1]

Another helpful sign of belonging to which Green calls attention is "a willingness to face the opposition of 'the world' (a technical term in the Johannine literature to indicate society which has left God out), and to get involved in the loving fellowship of the family of Christ."[2] And we are asked to note specifically what John observes on this point: "My brothers, do not be surprised if the world hates you. We for our part have crossed over from death to life; this we know, because we love our brothers" (1 John 3:13).

So the question of my belonging to God can be answered, in part at least, by an examination of my relationship to my fellow believers. We are at this point completing the circle and are coming back to the matter we have already discussed, namely, that of building up the church and working in the interest of the community of believers. Paul strongly underlines this consideration in his correspondence to the Corinthians. He indicates that it is a sign of being Spirit-filled.

5. The next point of entry in the Spirit's ministry is in giving to us Christ's righteousness, whether it comes to us as justification or as sanctification. Whatever difficulties we may have in defining each term, they are both of Christ. For years much tension and shouting have been in evidence among Christians over whether one is "declared" righteous or "made" righteous. (This is apart from the fact that only professionals or semiprofessionals seem to have any idea of what they mean anyway; and even then the wooliness can be incredible.) As a result, one wonders whether it is not high time to drop the terms and seek new and fresh ways of simply stating what happens when Jesus is accepted as Lord and Saviour. "Christ's righteousness for us"—is it legal or moral? imputed or imparted? (At which point one becomes either bored to death or heads for the dictionary.)

When I use the term "justification," I mean simply the experience of being accepted by God as a human being, warts and all. The term refers to the experience the Holy Spirit brings to me. It is one of coming out of the tunnel into daylight; out of suffocation into free and unlabored breathing; from being lost to being found; it means to be accepted.

Whatever you want to call that experience, it is something that is very important in the life of every reborn person. It meets a very basic need. It has to do with being alive and with feeling the energizing power of a new life. Its opposite is lostness, alienation, rejection, and meaninglessness. The very thought of these provokes an immediate chill. The ministry of the Spirit causes me to discover that in Christ the chill is gone and that the warmth which comes is not just some temporary kick, but is real and lasting. When this happens I begin to understand, maybe for the first time in my life, what it means to stand acquitted (Rom. 8:1) and, therefore, to be free (2 Cor. 3:17).

But this is the Spirit's point of entry. It is the beginning: Now a life remains to be lived. The Spirit who has given life has also come to dwell (Rom. 8:11). To be given life means to be given an opportunity to live and not to die upon birth. It is clearly the Spirit's intent that I shall not continue the kind of life I used to live (Gal. 2:20). I am now to walk in the Spirit. I am to turn my back on spiritual decay and death, and fight the remnants of it that may still linger with me (Gal. 5:24; 6:16). "If the Spirit is the source of our life, let the Spirit also direct our course" (Gal. 5:25).

This new life is one in which Christ's character is to be increasingly reflected in us. Again we see how the Spirit is concerned with our relationship with Christ. Colossians 3 brings out with particular clarity what this new life of the Spirit in Christ means. There we are told that since we now belong to Christ, His qualities of "compassion, kindness, humility, gentleness, patience" (verse 12) are to be reproduced in our lives. Well, are they? Again it is the Spirit and the Word that in the end must pass judgment on that by convicting us when we fail and assuring us when we succeed.

The process of reproducing Christ's character in our lives does not end until we see Him face-to-face. John said: "Here and now, dear friends, we are God's children; what we shall be has not yet been disclosed, but we know that when it is disclosed we shall be like him, because we shall see him as he is. Everyone who has this hope before him purifies himself, as Christ is pure" (1 John 3:2).

Referring collectively to the points of entry of the Spirit into the life of believers, the New Testament uses two words that we shall examine: "seal" and "pledge" (KJV, "earnest"). We note particularly Paul's use of these words in three different passages.

"And if you and we belong to Christ, guaranteed as his and anointed, it is all God's doing; it is God also who has set his seal upon us, and as a pledge of what is to come has given the Spirit to dwell in our hearts" (2 Cor. 1:21, 22).

"When you had heard the message of the truth, . . . and had believed it, [you] became incorporate in Christ and received the seal of the promised Holy Spirit; and that Spirit is the pledge that we shall enter upon our heritage" (Eph. 1:13, 14).

"Do not grieve the Holy Spirit of God, for that Spirit is the seal with which you were marked for the day of our final liberation" (Eph. 4:30).

Where does the idea of seal or sealing come from, and what does Paul mean by it in these passages?

The word was used widely in Greek commerce. In its secular context it meant to ratify, to give authority to, to guarantee, to mark ownership (as in branding slaves), or to attest. When a seal on a document was preserved intact, it served as proof that the document had not been tampered with.

In a religious context the concept of God setting a mark or seal upon people is not unique to the New Testament. In Ezekiel 9:3-6 the Lord calls a servant to go through Jerusalem and put a mark on the forehead of His faithful ones. Those so marked would be shielded on the day of vengeance. The parallel between this passage and Revelation 7:3 and 9:4 is unmistakable. Clearly here are individuals whom God claims ownership of. They have been sealed, and they are His. Also the followers of the beast (Rev. 13:16, 17) are "branded." The idea of ownership is just as emphatic here, although in this instance the persons owned belong to the forces opposed to God.

It is with this kind of background that we must understand Paul's idea of the sealing of God's people. They are "marked for the day of . . . final liberation." They are claimed by God as His, and this assures salvation. Furthermore, while we are not prepared to think of the "marking" of God's people in physical terms akin to the branding of cattle or to tribal marks incised on the forehead, there is nothing to suggest that it is mystical and invisible, any more than living a Christian life is invisible. As a rule, the direction of one's life is discernible. Signs of loyalties are being shown continuously, and if there is a shift in loyalty, signs of that shift surface as well. If one particular happening, habit, or phenomenon should come to be widely recognized as the sign of one's loyalty, then obviously it becomes very conspicuous and will no doubt also serve as a particular testing point not because it is necessarily more important than other signs of loyalty but because particular attention has been drawn to it. The same principle holds whether one's loyalty is to God or to the beast.

God gives to those "in Christ"—an expression of which Paul is particularly fond—a guarantee. It assures them that, assuming faithfulness, they will come through and that their mission, which is Christ's mission, will be successfully completed. Paul ties together these four expressions: guarantee, seal, anointing, and pledge. (The Greek word translated *pledge* means "first installment" or "down payment," which guarantees not only ownership but also that there is more to come.)

There has been much arguing as to whether Paul had Christian baptism in mind when he used these figures. I think there is little doubt that he did have baptism in mind, at least in the two Ephesian passages, and possibly also in 2 Corinthians 1:21, 22. But I believe it refers to baptism in the sense that we have previously spoken of it in our study, namely, as climax to "the whole complex of . . . [a believer's] entry into the Christian life—conversion, faith, baptism, the reception of the Spirit."[3]

Baptism in water comes, then, as the effective expression of what is a very profound inward experience. There is absolutely nothing to suggest that the anointing/sealing/pledging images of Paul point to any rite other than baptism in water (or the laying on of hands), nor do we find in the passages discussed early roots of the practice of confirmation. The latter has been very helpfully examined and dismissed by the Cambridge theologian G.W.H. Lampe in his book *The Seal of the Spirit.* To talk about confirmation is to read a much later post-apostolic occasional usage of the word "seal" back into the New Testament record. Such a practice, of course, is unacceptable.

What Paul wishes to say is that the Holy Spirit, expressing Himself in numerous ways, as we have indicated in our study, comes to us at the beginning of our life of commitment to Jesus Christ, that He identifies us as belonging to the Lord, and that His initial entry into the life promises and guarantees much more to come. It is in this sense that the Holy Spirit comes as "firstfruits of the harvest to come" (Rom. 8:23).

What happens if we have no particular interest in the "early harvest" and resist the ministry of the Spirit? We would be guilty of sin against the Holy Ghost, or what the New Testament speaks of as "grieving" or "blaspheming" God's Spirit. To do that spells death—spiritual death now and in a much more complete sense future eternal separation from God. We will note some of the New Testament passages that speak of this condition.

The earliest one is the statement of Jesus recorded by Mark: "I tell you this: no sin, no slander, is beyond forgiveness for men; but whoever slanders the Holy Spirit can never be forgiven; he is guilty of eternal sin" (Mark 3:29). The next verse makes it clear that Jesus made the statement because the leaders of the Jews declared Him to be possessed of an evil spirit. They claimed that He cast out demons by being in league with the prince of the demons. Although Jesus answered them plainly by showing how ridiculous such a claim was ("Evil casting out evil! Whoever heard of such a thing?"), "they were too proud to confess their error."[4]

In effect, they called Jesus Christ a liar. By doing this they rejected the convictions of the Holy Spirit that the Son of man was the Messiah. It was this rejection that Jesus calls sin against the Holy Spirit. The Jewish leaders knew that "divine power attended Christ, but in order to resist the truth, they attributed the work of the Holy Spirit to Satan. In doing this they deliberately chose deception."[5] To take such a position, deliberately and stubbornly, as did the Jewish leaders, is to place oneself outside God's salvation. Jesus Christ is God's only answer to the sin problem. Reject Him, as did the scribes on this occasion, and God has nothing further to offer.

Two occurrences recorded in the Old Testament provide us with a background against which to view the phenomenon of sin against the Holy Spirit. The first is Pharaoh's reaction to the plagues that fell on Egypt. His initial answer to Moses was, "Who is the Lord . . . that I should obey him and let Israel go?" (Ex. 5:2). In words of warning through Moses, God went a long way in answering his question but, stubbornly resisting, Pharaoh refused to recognize the Lord of Israel. The consequence was that with each fresh decision to resist the message of the warnings and plagues, the process of self-hardening advanced. The question "Who is the Lord that I should obey him?" which initially could have been a perfectly reasonable one showing an understandable ignorance, became a determined resistance to a God who made Himself increasingly better known. And in this respect the story of Pharaoh illustrates well the course of sinning against the Spirit of God: "Every rejection of light hardens the heart and darkens the understanding."[6]

The second illustration is found in a passage of Isaiah in which the prophet recounts "the Lord's acts of unfailing love" (Isa. 63:7). He asks the people to remember "all that the Lord has done for" them. He had led the nation out of Egypt, an event that was held up as the supreme example of God's ability to save. During the difficult years that followed, the Israelites were "like cattle moving down into a valley without stumbling, guided by the Spirit of the Lord" (verse 14), yet they "rebelled and grieved" the Spirit of their God (verse 10). The extent of their rebellion can be appreciated only when compared with what God had done for them. He had revealed Himself in words and deeds. He had displayed His lovingkindness seemingly without measure.

It is easy to see a parallel between the description of Isaiah 63 and the experience of Jesus delineated in Mark 3:29, 30. "His mighty works had already been made known. The demons recognized their master. But this new work of God was greeted in precisely the same way as the old. The people instead of welcoming it rebelled against it, and grieved [blasphemed] God's Holy Spirit."[7]

God has no answer beyond Jesus Christ. For those who display an attitude like that of the scribes or of Israel of old there remains only the question posed: How can we escape if we ignore a salvation as great as this? (See Heb. 2:3.)

A slightly different point is brought out by Matthew and Luke in their parallels to Mark 3:29, 30. Mark tells us that the scribes attacked Jesus, and the warning is given on that account. Matthew 12:31, 32 and Luke 12:10 say that to speak a word against the Son of man can be forgiven, but blasphemy against the Holy Spirit cannot be forgiven. To the casual reader it may appear that we are faced with a slight contradiction. But we are not; neither is there really any basic difference in meaning between the parallel accounts. The wording in Mark is a broad statement of principle. In bringing salvation to humanity the Spirit and Christ are inseparable. The Spirit brings Christ to us and reveals Him as Saviour. To resist the gift (Christ) is to resist the giver (the Holy Spirit). One cannot do this without excluding oneself from God's salvation.

However, in Matthew and Luke, as well as in Hebrews 6:4-6, the issue is presented with a slightly different point of emphasis. Christ must no doubt often have been aware of the casual bystanders on the fringes of His listeners who in ignorance dismissed Him and went undisturbed on their ways. They had no more than a superficial, passing impression of Him. Or perhaps their sole knowledge of Him came from rumors passed on by unsympathetic lips. They were not touched by Him and had no basis on which to relate themselves to Him. From such a distance, in ignorance, they no doubt often spoke frivolously of Him. "Speaking a word against the Son of man" by them could be forgiven.[8] They were outsiders still to be won to God's kingdom.

However, having been touched by and made sensitive to what God wants and to what He offers in Christ, there can be no retreat without peril to one's eternal life. Blasphemy against the Holy Spirit in this most primary sense is no sudden, precise event or moment. Drifting into self-hardening is a process that is "gradual, and almost imperceptible" in which "when one ray of light is disregarded, there is a partial benumbing of the spiritual perceptions, and the second revealing of light is less clearly discerned. So the darkness increases, until it is night in the soul."[9]

But one may also conceive of blasphemy against the Holy Spirit in a more secondary, though no less important, sense. Having been won for the kingdom, having been "enlightened," as Hebrews 6:4 puts it, having emerged from the twilight zone of bystanders into the disciple flock, then to resist the ongoing ministry of the Spirit in leading to a more complete understanding of the truth of our Lord, and to resist the Spirit's invitation to repent when we go astray, is tantamount to turning one's back on God's kingdom and walking out. And where one then goes there is no salvation. This is no doubt the point that was in the mind of Isaiah as well as the Lord in the above passages.

It is not as though there is a particular guilt that is too great for God's mercy. It is simply that God's final answer is Jesus Christ. Turn your back on Him, and there is nothing more that God can do. On the other hand, when we come to Him in the repentant spirit of Isaiah, confessing that our own righteousness is as a filthy rag, that we are the clay and would like the divine Potter to shape us (Isa. 64:6-8), we shall be amazed at what God can do and will do for us. He comes to His children with the assurance "I will heal their apostasy; of my own bounty will I love them" (Hosea 14:4).

[1] Michael Green, *I Believe in the Holy Spirit,* p. 77.

[2] *Ibid.*

[3] C. K. Barrett, *A Commentary on the Second Epistle to the Corinthians,* Black's New Testament Commentary Series (London: Adam & Charles Black, 1973), p. 81.

[4] Ellen G. White, *The Desire of Ages,* p. 322.

[5] *Ibid.,* p. 323.

[6] *The Seventh-day Adventist Bible Commentary,* Ellen G. White Comments, vol. 1, p. 1100.

[7] Barrett, *The Holy Spirit and the Gospel Tradition,* p. 105.

[8] White, *The Desire of Ages,* p. 322.

[9] *Ibid.*

CHAPTER 7

Growing in the Spirit

Someone might comment: "If it's true that I received the gift of the Holy Spirit in my conversion experience when I made a full surrender to Jesus Christ, why is my spiritual life in no better state than it is at this moment? My pet sins of five years ago are relentlessly plaguing me! Why am I not gaining the victories I long for? Why don't I find more of the fruit of the Spirit appearing in my life? The same basic questioning keeps returning in different forms, and I find no rest. I'm unable to reconcile the belief that Christ's Spirit is with me with the shambles of my present life, although on reflection I don't suppose that I would be asking these questions were it not for the presence of the Spirit. Nevertheless, something is clearly wrong. It's obvious that I have not 'arrived' where I should be spiritually."

Yes, something is clearly wrong. But does the fault lie with either the absence of God's Spirit or His slowness in making available the full power of the Spirit? We closed one of our earlier chapters by saying categorically that spiritual failures in the lives of God's people lie with the people and not with God. This point we need to explore further.

When we gave our hearts to Jesus Christ, many of us thought that this would clear up all our problems. It was quite a shock to wake up and discover that what we had expected didn't happen. So what can we do? Many, maybe particularly the young and the very sensitive, will conclude: "Well, I guess I just wasn't converted! I guess I had everyone fooled, including myself!"

But that just is not true. Conversion, at which time we accept the Lord Jesus Christ and receive the gift of His Spirit, is not qualified by the immediate success or feebleness of our Christian performance. Conversion simply means that through the patient and, in the case of many, long wooing of God's Spirit,[1] we have come to the point where we are prepared to make one very fundamental decision: "I'm through with my old life! I'm going to stop fighting Jesus Christ! I'm going to join Him!"

In Romans 6 Paul lingers with beauty and clarity on this radical decision in which we turn our backs on one way of life and begin to walk in a new direction into a new kind of life. In one sense there is a feeling of arrival in that we who had previously been adrift have now found firm footing. We who had previously lived by substitutes have now found the real thing.

Yet any sense of arrival is completely overshadowed by a feeling of beginning. Something new is happening! "New thoughts, new feelings, new motives, are implanted."[2] From now on a whole new life is to be lived, and we have to learn how to live it. For most of us this takes time.

Let us have patience, tolerance, and compassion toward those newly born who find it difficult to learn to live afresh and to walk with any degree of steadiness. We ourselves stand in need of the same kind of compassion, because most of us have our off days. The spiritual "blueness" of Monday mornings is not easy to come to grips with, especially for those young and sensitive who become extremely distressed by their own spiritual condition and are prone to draw the wrong conclusions. It is possible to feel totally unprepared to face the week ahead. Distress and a feeling of hopelessness can be devastating and cause not a few to drift into indifference with a shrug. ("It isn't going to work anyway.") And then maybe some—yes, even Seventh-day Adventist young people—instead of going the way of indifference will seek emotionalism, sensationalism, or special manifestations of the Spirit in order to feel that power is within reach for snap victories over sins.

Both these ways are failures of faith. The former is a failure to understand growth in Christ, and the latter a failure to accept the assurance of Jesus that, while the Spirit is a stranger to the world, to you who have made the decision of your life He is known "because he dwells with you and is in you" (John 14:17).

So, what are we really saying? That once we have made our decision, that's it? That once we have received the initial gift of the Spirit, we've got it all and there is nowhere further to go? I know not how to give as emphatic a *no* as is needed to these questions. Were it otherwise, our hopelessness would be legitimate. But the very opposite is true. What has happened is that we have just been born (again); the Spirit of life has just come to dwell within. Now ahead lies a complete life of growing, in which we continuously and with an ever-increasing capacity draw on and make use of the Spirit's presence and power.

What is necessary is that we be able, on the one hand, to understand that the Spirit (not just fragments of Him) really comes to us individually when we begin life in God, that He is truly there and is not playing a spiritual game of hide-and-seek. On the other hand, we need to accept the reality of growing in the Spirit from where we stand today to ever-new heights and fulfillments.

A simple illustration that the famous evangelical preacher John R. W. Stott, former rector of All Souls Church, London, once gave states the point well. "Let us compare two people. One is a baby, newborn and weighing 7 pounds, who has just begun to breathe; the other is a full-grown man, 6 feet in height and 12 stone [168 lbs.] in weight. Both are fit and healthy; both are breathing properly; and both may be described as 'filled with air.' What, then, is the difference between them? It lies in the capacity of their lungs. Both are 'filled,' yet one is more filled than the other because his capacity is so much greater."[3]

There is no doubt a direct relationship between the Spirit's power in the life and our own ability to reflect His presence and utilize it. How does growth in this area come about?

It would be such a simple thing (to many probably both appealing and understandable) were we able to state unequivocally that growth in the Spirit comes about by self-discipline and the exercise of willpower. And surely it is beyond question that both of these play a vital role in Christian growth and in perfecting character. Were they, however, to be submitted as the answer to our question, we would have ample ground for despair. In no time at all we would know what it means to "flog a dead horse." Only arrogance and conceit could possibly prevent us from confessing our total inadequacy.

This statement by the Lord's servant answers our question: "Divine grace is needed at the beginning, divine grace at every step of advance, and divine grace alone can complete the work. . . .

" 'Ask ye of the Lord rain in the time of the latter rain.' Do not rest satisfied that in the ordinary course of the season, rain will fall. Ask for it. The growth and perfection of the seed rests not with the husbandman. God alone can ripen the harvest. But man's cooperation is required."[4]

The Galatian community had gone adrift regarding the adequacy of God's answer in Jesus Christ. And Paul provided a stinging rebuke by posing some very pointed questions: "You stupid Galatians! You must have been bewitched—you before whose eyes Jesus Christ was openly displayed upon his cross! Answer me one question: did you receive the Spirit by keeping the law or by believing the gospel message? Can it be that you are so stupid? You started with the spiritual; do you now look to the material to make you perfect? Have all your great experiences been in vain?" (Gal. 3:1-4).

Every age has had its own perversion of what spiritual fullness is. In Galatia and Colosse there were strains of legalism and Gnosticism to supplement God's answer in Jesus Christ so as to make it adequate. In certain charismatic communities it is supplemented by additional spiritual "techniques," a "deeper" message, or a "fuller" gospel (for instance, the Full Gospel Church or the Full Gospel Business Men's Association). To accept it as a fact that God has adequately met our needs in the gift of His Son, Jesus Christ, is for many too difficult (or perhaps too simple). And so off one goes, looking for supplements.

But God's adequate provision is never administered in a sovereign fashion. It demands an intense, determined, and full-time involvement of the recipient. "Man's cooperation is required." This is where willpower comes in. It is impossible to realize life goals in any area (we can inherit only so much!) without some self-discipline and the exercise of willpower. This is an intrinsic part of living a full life. Let us not pretend that discipline and willpower are hidden phenomena that are aroused from a deep slumber and caused to function in a religious context only. They are vital parts of the dynamics of responsive and responsible living. Therefore, obviously and naturally we cannot lead lives responsive to God and our fellow humans without exercising these powers. That need not be established as if it were an incredible or exceptional thing.

However, one common point in the above two quotations is that *as we began* (by "divine grace" or by "believing the gospel") so we are to *keep on* moving toward the ultimate fulfillment in the return of our Lord, always finding new fulfillments. *At no stage of our Christian growth does the method change.*

In his first letter John repeatedly emphasizes the two aspects that we also must insist on: (1) that Jesus Christ is the complete answer ("He who possesses the Son has life indeed" [1 John 5:12]); and (2) that to be involved with Him has practical consequences ("Whoever claims to be dwelling in him, binds himself to live as Christ himself lived" [1 John 2:6]). Growing in the Spirit depends on accepting these two. There are no further additions.

Let me reemphasize the point we have made several times in this study, namely, that the question of Spirit-baptism is synonymous with the question of the place and role of Jesus Christ in our lives. The lesson that comes to us from the well-known words of Jesus recorded in John 7:37-39 is that to thirst, to believe, to come, and to drink is an ongoing process. There is no once-for-all deposit at the beginning of the Christian walk. We need to keep coming back—for more.

Neither is it adequate to view the gift of the Spirit as a two-tier happening: one at the planting of the seed—the "early rain"—and the other to ripen the crop for the harvest—the "latter rain," although in a sense that we shall note below, such a distinction has validity. What we are objecting to is not only the unlikely idea of a God-intended barrenness between two "deposits," but the whole suggestion that it should be possible to collect "manna" for future use.

One may well store material things for a variety of personal seven lean years, but spirituality is not a storable quantity. And dry spells are themselves evidence of the fact. It is in this sense, after observing that "Christ was *continually* receiving from the Father," that Ellen G. White says: "Daily He received a fresh baptism of the Holy Spirit."[5] (The expression "baptism of the Holy Spirit" was used before the charismatic movements of today or even before historic Pentecostalism came along and gave it a slanted content. This daily baptism is synonymous with our growing in the Spirit.)

Not only Christ was to have this experience "daily," or continuously, but also God's children should see it as "their privilege to receive every day the baptism of the Holy Spirit."[6] "God desires to refresh His people by the gift of the Holy Spirit, baptizing them anew in His love. There is no need for a dearth of the Spirit in the church."[7]

With an eye to the wording in John 7, this continuous appropriation of the Spirit requires a definite awareness of need ("thirst"), taking the specific steps of coming and "drinking" through the reading of the Word, meditation, prayer, and through decision-making evidenced in the way we live our lives.

The Spirit is not someone to be received and kept for ourselves. His continuous indwelling will cause an equally continuous flowing forth in worship, fellowship, service, and witnessing. Not only does the Holy Spirit sustain our relationship with God and our fellow human beings, but He is also the one without whom we could not even begin to understand what such a relationship has to offer and where it may take us.

As 1 Corinthians 13 teaches with clarity and great beauty, the spiritual growth to which we are referring means to come increasingly to grips with the natural problem of self-assertion. It means to seek tirelessly the interest of God and other people. "Proexistence" is the word. The extent of that growth other people will without doubt be able to judge better than we ourselves. But when it does begin, not only our relationships to God and other people will be radically affected, but also our relationships to material things. Viewpoints will change, goals and ambitions will be reshaped, and "political exercises" and concerns will lose their attraction.

Those who heed Paul's admonition to "let the Holy Spirit fill you" (Eph. 5:18) become in their lives bearers of fruit that somehow seem unnatural. The fruit appears so different because it is distinct from that which previously came all too naturally. We must accept the fact that to walk in the Spirit is hallmarked less by charismatic elation and more by moral qualities. "If you are guided by the Spirit you will not fulfil the desires of your lower nature. That nature sets its desires against the Spirit, while the Spirit fights against it" (Gal. 5:16, 17).

Paul gives us such a clear contrast between the works of the corrupt nature ("flesh") and the fruit of the Spirit (verses 19-25) as to make it absolutely plain to any honest seeker that to be filled with the Spirit has to do with morality and the way in which we exist in our daily lives. Again a statement by Stott: "The real proof of a deep work of the Spirit of God in any human being is neither subjective, emotional experiences, nor spectacular signs, but moral, Christlike qualities. Here is a Christian who makes great claims in the realm of experience, but lacks love, joy, peace, kindness and self-control: I think all of us will say that there is something wrong with his claims."[8]

Furthermore, as Paul proceeds to point out in Galatians 6, we reap fruit of the Spirit only if that is the kind of seed we have been sowing. We are involved not only in harvesting but in sowing as well. If we sow seeds of corruption and decay and keep on feeding what Paul in this passage calls the "lower nature," we can hardly expect the fruit of the Spirit. The experience of many of us is, I fear, that we consistently sow seeds of decay and then, in prayer, ask God somehow to cause the fruit of the Spirit to appear. That, says Paul (Gal. 6:7, 8), is an impossibility.

At no point in our lives does this process of sowing and reaping stop. At no point does the development of character stop. Growth in grace is the work of a lifetime.[9] This growing in the Spirit in righteousness, sanctification, perfection, maturity—help yourself to the label that is clearest to you—is an increasing realization of the potentials that a life in Christ has to offer. It is a constant reaching upward, finding ever new heights. It is also a growth in dependence on our Lord, never in the direction of independence and self-sufficiency. Jesus' warning that unless we remain united with Him we become as dead branches and are treated as such (John 15:1-6) strikes home with increasing force.

One final point about sowing: While we are continually harvesting a Christian character ("fruit of the Spirit") in this life, our ultimate harvest of an eternal life is no less dependent on the kind of seed we are sowing daily. The morality and direction of our everyday lives shapes our eternity.

Now let's go back to a point we said we would return to, namely, viewing the descent of the Holy Spirit as "early rain" and "latter rain." The images of the "early" and "latter" rain—in Palestine the former fell at the time of sowing to cause the seed to germinate, and the latter to ripen it for the harvest—appropriately symbolize the work of the Holy Spirit. The prophet Isaiah wrote: "I will pour down rain on a thirsty land, showers on the dry ground. I will pour out my Spirit on your offspring and my blessing on your children" (Isa. 44:3).

And Zechariah, clearly having something more than physical rain in mind, encouraged the people to "ask of the Lord rain in the autumn [which was the time for sowing in Palestine], ask him for rain in the spring . . . and he will give you showers of rain" (Zech. 10:1).

Another prophet admonished: "Come, let us return to the Lord. . . . Let us humble ourselves, let us strive to know the Lord, whose justice dawns like morning light, and its dawning is as sure as the sunrise. It will come to us like a shower, like spring rains that water the earth" (Hosea 6:1-3).

The prophet Joel referred to God as the one who "has given the early rain for your vindication, he has poured down for you abundant rain, the early and the latter rain" (Joel 2:23, RSV). He then went on to utter the prophecy that Peter, on the day of Pentecost, says was being fulfilled right then: "Thereafter the day shall come when I will pour out my spirit on all mankind; your sons and your daughters shall prophesy" (verse 28).

Notice that there is nothing in Peter's words or elsewhere in the New Testament to suggest that Joel's original prophecy was exhausted in the fulfillment at Pentecost. On the contrary, Pentecost initiated an age marked by the newness and freshness of the Holy Spirit's ministry, which has never ceased.

As already noted several times, Paul wrote not only of fruit that the Spirit would cause to appear, but also of special gifts that He would give to various individuals to meet the needs of the church in the time between the ascension of Jesus Christ and His return. In what sense, then, can one speak of specific "early" and "latter" rains of the Spirit?

There is first of all an objective or historical phase that should be considered. Though God's Spirit had always been present with His people, He came specifically at Pentecost in the sense that He inaugurated a new ministry, namely, that of communicating the gospel of salvation in Jesus Christ. *That* He has never stopped doing. And there is no inspired word that He will suspend these activities or withdraw and hold Himself in abeyance, "gathering strength" as it were (if I may be excused for appearing casual) for a final pouring out of Himself at the very end of time to wind it all up. As long as the work of reconciliation goes on, the Spirit is here to interpret the gospel and to give force to its proclamation. Only the end of the ministry of reconciliation will cause the Spirit to terminate His work.

The Spirit, who was present with the people before Pentecost, came then at a specific time in history to give impetus to the beginning of the Christian ministry. So He who has been present and active in the church since then will come and display His power in even more remarkable ways than at Pentecost,[10] to bring the work of reconciliation to its final consummation.

No less than a powerful display of God's power was needed at the beginning of Christianity to verify that God was in it. No less than the greatest display of the same power and of the presence of the Spirit will be needed on the eve of our Lord's return to penetrate an increasingly hostile darkness and make contact with men and women yet to be claimed for God—souls who are bewildered, afraid, groping about for hope and security. Again, nothing less than a powerful demonstration will be needed to show that God is still in this movement among His people and that He will see them through the difficult last days. It would only be in this sense that one could speak of an "early" and a "latter" rain of the Spirit as points in history.

However, we must hasten to add that in this latter rain, just prior to the coming of our Lord, the Spirit does not come as a stranger or as one who has been absent. We must resist the kind of two-tier system suggesting a vacuum between the two points. There is an unbroken continuity between the ministry of the Spirit as "early rain" and as "latter rain."

The sigh from the lips of some that, alas, the Spirit is not present with God's people today as He ought to be should more correctly be that God's people are not with the Spirit today as they ought to be. Some people's understanding of the latter rain has received an unfortunate twist in which God is presented as holding back His Spirit.

Some Christians even assume that *He* must be worked on and persuaded to release the Spirit. The thought suggests that the spiritual shortcomings of God's people today are because they have not received the outpouring of the latter rain. Insidiously, the blame is thus shifted to God, and we sit back waiting for Him to take the initiative in correcting things by pouring out the latter rain of the Spirit.

This kind of thinking is totally false. The blame for the present state of God's people lies with them, not with Him. Ellen G. White penned many a counsel on this point, of which the church should take serious note. In them she calls attention to a subjective phase of an early and a latter rain in which there must be equal continuity between the two in our personal experiences. Note the following on *growing* in the Spirit: "The ripening of the grain represents the completion of the work of God's grace in the soul. . . . The latter rain, ripening earth's harvest, represents the spiritual grace that prepares the church for the coming of the Son of man. But unless the former rain has fallen, there will be no life; the green blade will not spring up."[11]

"Many have in a great measure failed to receive the former rain. They have not obtained all the benefits that God has thus provided for them. They expect that the lack will be supplied by the latter rain. When the richest abundance of grace shall be bestowed, they intend to open their hearts to receive it. They are making a terrible mistake. *The work that God has begun in the human heart in giving His light and knowledge must be continually going forward.*"[12]

"We must not wait for the latter rain. It is coming upon all who will recognize and appropriate the dew and showers of grace that fall upon us. . . . When we appreciate the sure mercies of God, who loves to have us trust Him, then every promise will be fulfilled."[13]

"I have no specific time of which to speak when the outpouring of the Holy Spirit [as latter rain] will take place . . . ; my message is that our only safety is in being ready for the heavenly refreshing, *having our lamps trimmed and burning.*"[14]

And finally: "I saw that many were neglecting the preparation so needful and were looking to the time of 'refreshing' and the 'latter rain' to fit them to stand in the day of the Lord and to live in His sight. Oh, how many I saw in the time of trouble without a shelter! They had neglected the needful preparation, therefore they could not receive the refreshing that all must have to fit them to live in the sight of a holy God. . . . I saw that none could share the 'refreshing' unless they obtain the victory over every besetment, over pride, selfishness, love of the world, and over every wrong word and action. *We should, therefore, be drawing nearer and nearer to the Lord.*"[15]

The one point that she drives home with considerable force in these statements is that in order to receive the latter rain we must continually grow in the Spirit, constantly "going forward." We must keep our "lamps trimmed and burning" perpetually, and become involved in the process of being drawn "nearer and nearer to the Lord."

Sitting back awaiting the arrival of some Stranger or of some God-sent secret antidote to sin will in the end prove to have been a useless exercise. To obey God, to grow in the Spirit, to come, to thirst, and to drink is a present experience that must be utilized to the full *now!* Only thus is there any assurance that we shall receive more. Put simply, the idea of "more" is that of progression or forward and upward movements to greater heights, more strength, further victories. We cannot receive *more* unless we already possess *some.*

Very few of us are really exploring the ultimate potential that a life in Christ has to offer. Few of us are able to speak from experience of what it means to grow in the Spirit. Yet this is no different from growing in commitment to Jesus Christ. Spiritual growth is conditioned by the extent to which we are "drawing nearer and nearer to the Lord."

Most of us are, I fear, spiritual daydreamers, who have adopted a relaxed posture while we await the day when God shall set all things right. What a disappointment we face! There will be nothing for us to receive. Only to those who appreciate and appropriate the potentials of a present experience with God will "every promise . . . be fulfilled."

Growing is something that has to be worked on. The counsel is to "be fervent in prayer and watch in the Spirit."[16] That cannot be the experience of those to whom the Spirit is yet to come.

---

[1] This is beautifully described in *The Desire of Ages,* pp. 167-177, and commented on in the story of the leaven in *Christ's Object Lessons,* pp. 95-102.

[2] Ellen G. White, *Christ's Object Lessons,* p. 98.

[3] John R. W. Stott, *Baptism and Fullness: The Work of the Holy Spirit,* p. 61.

[4] Ellen G. White, *Testimonies to Ministers,* p. 508.

[5] ———, *Christ's Object Lessons,* p. 139.

[6] ———, *Counsels to Parents and Teachers* (Mountain View, Calif.: Pacific Press Pub. Assn.), p. 131.

[7] ———, *Testimonies,* vol. 9, p. 40.

[8] Stott, p. 79.

[9] Ellen G. White, *The Acts of the Apostles,* p. 560.

[10] *The Seventh-day Adventist Bible Commentary,* Ellen G. White Comments, vol. 6, p. 1055.

[11] White, *Testimonies to Ministers,* p. 506.

[12] *Ibid.,* p. 507. (Italics supplied.)

[13] *The Seventh-day Adventist Bible Commentary,* Ellen G. White Comments, vol. 7, p. 984.

[14] *Ibid.* (Italics supplied.)

[15] Ellen G. White, *Early Writings* (Washington, D.C.: Review and Herald Pub. Assn.), p. 71. (Italics supplied.)

[16] ———, *Testimonies to Ministers,* p. 512. (Italics supplied.)

CHAPTER 8

The Community of the Spirit

The prospect of Christ leaving His disciples after three and a half years of friendship, fellowship, instruction, and sharing of life must have caused considerable concern among His immediate followers. What would become of them when He was gone? While genuine and sincere, they seemed so fickle and so unsure; so unpredictable and so ill-prepared to stand firmly for what they had come to know as truth. They knew the truth, but would they be able to keep it in focus also when he was gone?

I remember the words of a Tubingen theologian about the resurrection of Jesus: "It happened so long ago that it is hardly true anymore." Can one survive as a believer also when a long time passes between the promises and their fulfillment? Will it all stay sharp and in focus, or will it all seem a bit unreal? Would the disciples survive and be true to Him on their own? Or is it possible that they would in fact never be on their own?

At various times Jesus tried to prepare them for the fact that He would be leaving (for example, Matt. 26:11; John 7:33, 34). Somehow they had to come to terms with that reality soon. The journeys they had made together would end. They would not continue to talk together and pray together as they had for three and a half years. They would not see Him or touch Him, simply because He would not be there. He would be gone!

To prepare them for that potentially traumatic moment Jesus assured them that although He would physically leave them, He would never really leave them. "I am with you always, to the very end of the age" (Matt. 28:20, NIV). "I will not leave you as orphans; I will come to you" (John 14:18, NIV). God would take an initiative that would maintain an unbroken continuity with the person and mission of Jesus Christ. Christ's ascension would not end God's literal and real presence among humanity. It would simply enter a new phase.

Fulfillment, as we have stated repeatedly in this study, was to come in the gift of the Holy Spirit, and He would continuously be present with the believers as long as God is engaged in the business of saving people. Pentecost marked the beginning of this new chapter.

Of course the Holy Spirit as the third person of the Godhead had been present and active among us since the beginning of time. However little the Jews of the Old Testament times had been able to conceive of God in Trinitarian terms—their belief was simply that "The Lord our God, the Lord is one" (Deut. 6:4, NIV)—yet, as one reads the Old Testament through the events of the New Testament the Spirit was clearly there from Creation onward. He was there inspiring the prophets (1 Kings 22:24; 2 Sam. 23:2; Isa. 61:1; Eze. 11:5; Micah 3:8) and providing the gift of leadership to the judges (Judges 3:10; 11:29). He was there as the one who creates out of nothing, whether we see Him in the Genesis creation account or in the re-creation vision of Ezekiel 37. Humanity's natural origin is neither the dust of the earth nor bleached bones. It is God who creates, and He said to the prophet: "I will put my spirit into you and you shall live" (Eze. 37:14).

Through His Spirit God has since the beginning of time been at work creating and re-creating, designing and restoring. The community of God's people has always been the community of the Spirit. This is where He is and where He functions. "The Spirit recreates, refines, and sanctifies human beings, fitting them to become members of the royal family."[1]

But when we come to the community of believers *after* the ascension of Christ, it is clear that a new "epoch of the Spirit" was to begin. He was to take on a set of functions among the believers and in the community that had not been seen before, at least not in quite that manner. Jesus, on whom the Holy Spirit was present without measure, taught His followers that after His own death and ascension something special would happen. The Spirit would come to the community of believers in a way they had not previously been accustomed to and in a role He had not had before. He would have a role and an assignment that would be particularly linked to the person and message of Jesus Christ.

Therefore, this could begin only after Christ's ascension. The Spirit would then display His presence in a variety of gifts and functions. These gifts and functions were designed to help the community of believers remember and understand Jesus' teachings, equipping them to lead lives of discipleship and witness to those who did not know Jesus Christ and had not accepted Him as Lord and Saviour. In Jesus' parting message to His disciples as recorded in John 14-16, He tells them about the coming of the Spirit and what the Spirit would do.

One of the difficulties that the community of God's children was—and is—faced with after the ascension of Jesus Christ is the passing of time so that Jesus' messages might not seem as sharp and clear as they once were. This may not be so much a matter of apostasy as it is the human frailty of a dimmed vision and failing memory.

Each generation of believers lives in expectation of and

with a deep longing for the return of the Lord, as He promised. But they will at times be perplexed by the apparent delay. So much time seems to pass. Is there something else that must happen before the Lord can return? Events will happen in history and on the secular scene that the believers will search the Scriptures to find meaning for. The believing mind turns to the prophetic and apocalyptic messages of the Bible to discover whether other events are foretold by inspired writers, which to the believers will be signposts or milestones on the journey to the Promised Land. How can the believer be sure that the interpretations arrived at are reliable and safe? The presence of the Holy Spirit makes it possible. He is the only safe guide.

Furthermore, contemporary thought is constantly inviting all to reflect the culture in which they find themselves both in terms of values and lifestyle. And yet the believers know that God has already laid down the values that apply and the quality of life that Christians are to espouse and follow. How can God's children be sure that they do not come adrift in these matters? How can they know that they take their directions from God and not from contemporary culture?

Again, the presence of the Holy Spirit is the answer. He is given to serve the needs of the church in these matters. He is present among believers to guide, remind, and teach them. "By [the Holy Spirit's] power the vital truths upon which the salvation of the soul depends are impressed upon the mind, and the way of life is made so plain that none need err therein."[2]

He is also the enabling force that equips God's people to function as believers. "When by the Holy Spirit divine truths are impressed upon the heart, new conceptions are awakened, and the energies hitherto dormant are aroused to cooperate with God."[3]

The continuity between Jesus Christ in person and the

Holy Spirit is clear. It is as though Christ is saying: "I told you then . . . (when I was physically present among you), and I am telling you now . . . (by the presence of the Spirit)."

Jesus made a solemn promise that a new epoch of the Spirit would soon come. The Father was committed to making a special endowment of the Spirit to the believers. Jesus said one day to His disciples: "If you then, though you are evil, know how to give good gifts to your children, how much more will your Father in heaven give the Holy Spirit to those who ask him!" (Luke 11:13, NIV). Jesus, on inviting those who were thirsty to come to Him and drink, quoted Isaiah 58:11: "The Lord will be your guide continually and will satisfy your needs, . . . You will be like a well-watered garden, like a spring whose waters never fail." Then the text reads: "By this he meant the Spirit, whom those who believed in him were later to receive. Up to that time the Spirit had not been given, since Jesus had not yet been glorified" (John 7:39, NIV). Clearly something of greatest importance for the spiritual welfare and effectiveness of the community of believers was about to happen. The thought of a special coming of the Spirit marks that beginning.

The gift of the Holy Spirit makes the difference! If the Spirit were not present among us today we would have no message to bring. We could relate some stories and tell of some interesting events, yes, but some of these on their own would not make up the gospel, and salvation would not come from them.

The role of the Holy Spirit is closely linked to the person and mission of Jesus Christ. The gift of the Holy Spirit is to make otherwise frail human beings into a genuine community of Christ's disciples. The spiritual gifts are to equip that community to function for Christ. Whereas the various gifts of the Spirit are given as God deems necessary and by His choice, the primary *gift* of the Holy Spirit is given to all who are genuinely committed to Jesus Christ and obeying Him. Paul, writing to a church that was greatly divided over spiritual gifts, made the point that all who have accepted Jesus Christ as their personal Saviour and have by baptism been brought into the body of Christ, which is the church, have this in common: The one Holy Spirit has been poured out for them to drink (1 Cor. 12:13). They have had "a taste of the heavenly gift" and "a share in the Holy Spirit" (Heb. 6:4).

One can well understand that some will find this difficult to grasp and accept. We may have been brought up to think that the gift of the Spirit belongs to an advanced, maybe more successful stage of our Christian journey, when the mistakes, with which our individual lives are sprinkled, are finished—well, maybe not entirely, but at least we live better lives. We don't make the mistakes we once used to. And growth of this kind is normal; one would expect it to happen. It is a growth in the Spirit and a growth in Christ, and it is right. It must happen.

And yet, there is another reality that is also clear. Sinfulness does not readily give up its cohabitation in the body that now belongs to Christ and to which the Spirit has come as a gift. We are, as believers, covered by the righteousness of Christ, while at the same time the presence of sin manifests itself in our lives. This tension is a reality that we all live with and struggle with and cannot deny! That is the way our humanity is. However, that does not mean that the Holy Spirit is a stranger to us. The wonderful news is that it is possible to grow in the Spirit. It is possible to leave behind life patterns and mistakes of the past, but throughout this growing, life-changing development we belong to Christ. We are covered by His righteousness. The fact is that were it not for the presence of the Spirit in our lives we would not recognize the mistakes of the past as flaws in need of forgiveness and repair.

Paul is emphatic. It is not possible to be a believer—a follower of Christ—without the presence of the Spirit (Rom. 8:9).

Another important point that Paul makes is: "The Spirit himself testifies with our spirit that we are God's children" (verse 16, NIV). He is there to make us sure. I am meant to be able to say not just that I hope that I am a child of God but that I *know* I am.

The outpouring of the Holy Spirit on the community of believers, as well as the manifestation of various gifts of the Spirit, are all "given for the common good" (1 Cor. 12:7, NIV). Practically, what does that mean for us today?

1. Spiritual gifts are practical; they are for the good of the people. They are not meant as a private endowment given to an individual isolated from the community. Rather, it is all about the ability to function as a member of a larger body to whom a mission has been given. To live a spiritual life is therefore a very practical matter. And only those who are prepared to engage themselves practically can discover the reality of what it means to live by the Spirit. Being a Christian is best defined in what one does for others. (See Eph. 4:12.)

And therefore, all of us must ask ourselves: What am I doing? What occupies the days of my week? What do I call important? Does the quality of life of other people become better because I am there? Or is it possible that my presence has no practical consequence in the lives of other people? The Holy Spirit's presence is meant to be a catalyst for change.

2. The gift of the Spirit is linked to "power from above" (Luke 24:49). Spiritfilledness is the opposite of weakness, lethargy, and confusion. It has to do with power to be and to act, and it lifts us to a level where we otherwise would not be. And this power is nothing other than the power of creation. It is the power to take that which

is not and make something of wonder and beauty. And as we look at ourselves, do we not find cause to be thankful for the fact that God creates out of nothing? When all is said and done, what do we have to offer, except a willing heart that has been surrendered to Jesus Christ? That very same reality was what Pentecost signified. The Creator-Spirit took a group of uncertain, frightened, and discouraged individuals and made them into witnesses who could go forth with unstoppable conviction and motivation. It was the Spirit who did it—and who does it today.

3. The Spirit was given to make one people—one family—out of many individuals and unite them in peace (Eph. 4:3), without division (1 Cor. 1:10) and who love one another. When that happens the climate in the church becomes such that individuals want to belong and make it their home. The church is meant to offer a "consumer-friendly" environment, especially to those whose battle scars are visible.

It is no coincidence that the fruit of the Spirit finds its meaning only in relationships with other people (Gal. 5:22; Eph. 4:32). It is also no coincidence that the chapter on love (1 Cor. 13) is placed in the middle of Paul's treatment of spiritual gifts. The unity in the church is organic; life and nurture is to flow from one individual to the next. That is the meaning of being one "body." It is the Spirit who binds us together.

And here I must pause and ask myself: What is it that comes from me and is shared with my brothers and sisters in the church? Is it something that gives life, hope, encouragement, a reason to go on, or is it discouraging, negative, critical, cynical, and ultimately destructive of life itself?

Spirituality is always a very practical matter, and it always has practical consequences. So it is for us today. Instead of living in the hope that one day the Spirit will come also to me, I can live today fully as the Spirit who is with me makes possible now. Instead of living with a dream and hope, which we also do, I learn to live with some spiritual realities that are here now. Out of that comes a strong and attractive Christian life.

---

[1] E. G. White, *Gospel Workers,* p. 287.
[2] ———, *Christ's Object Lessons,* p. 113.
[3] ———, *Acts of the Apostles,* p. 520.

CHAPTER 9

The Holy Spirit and the World

What does God think of the world? The question itself may strike not a few as both impudent and presumptuous. And they may feel that an attempt to answer it, particularly when those who try are committed Christians who believe that God has a very special interest in them and others similarly committed, is a galling display of arrogance. The lifted finger drives the accusation home: How dare you make pronouncements about what God thinks of the world (or, for that matter, of anyone except possibly yourself when you confess your own faith)—you who are manifestly hostile to the world?

The danger of arrogance does not lie in my confessing what I believe to be God's interest in me and to my own interest in Him. Rather, it is found in my presuming that I can make an accurate statement about His interest in others who may not be committed as I am, or who express their commitment in ways not immediately familiar to me.

So we cringe under the weight of that awareness. Even so, we feel that we should not leave the subject of the Holy Spirit entirely without reflecting for a moment on God's interest in the world—and we do so with a prayerful sigh for the grace of humility.

What do we understand by the expression "the world"? Is it geography, space, demography, ethnic and linguistic divisions, or organizations and structures? Since we are inquiring into *God's* interest in the world, we must obviously first of all come to an understanding of what the Bible means by "the world."

The casual understanding that many Christians have of the world, particularly as some impressions from John 17 pass quickly before them, is that the world is evil and does not know God (verse 25). As it hated Christ, so it will also hate those who follow Him (verse 14). God, consequently, has a very disapproving opinion of the world. But such a perspective is too limited to help anyone, least of all Christians who are concerned with God's mission in the world today. We must search for a more comprehensive understanding.

We need immediately to rule out Gnostic and Hellenistic ideas that material things are inherently evil and that, therefore, the material world is intrinsically evil. The Bible gives no support to that kind of thinking. The world is part of God's creation. It is part of that which He initially pronounced good. And despite what has happened since, there is still much in it that is good (Gen. 1:31; John 1:3; Acts 17:24; Rom. 1:20).

In the Bible we meet a second concept of the world, kosmos, in which the emphasis is on the individuals who inhabit this space, namely, humankind. This view looms large in the biblical picture. *Kosmos* is preeminently "the world of men and human affairs . . . a world capable of knowing, or of reprehensively not knowing, its Maker."[1] The fourth Gospel speaks with particular clarity: "God loved the world so much that he gave his only Son, that everyone who has faith in him may not die but have eternal life" (John 3:16). Although the world as a whole "did not recognize him" (John 1:10), there were some who saw and clearly confessed that He was "the Saviour of the world" (John 4:42)—the One who had come to "[take] away the sin of the world" (John 1:29) and bring "life to the world" (John 6:33). Motivated by love (John 3:16), God is presented as one who is enormously sensitive to the needs of humanity. The physical arrangements and structures were in themselves no goal. God placed supreme value on *humankind,* and the space was provided for the benefit of humanity.

The third underlying idea in the biblical understanding of *kosmos* is that of a creation that has gone wrong, which harbors evil and represents opposition to God ("The whole godless world lies in the power of the evil one" [1 John 5:19]). "Hence there arises the distinctive New Testament sense of *kosmos* as the world over against God, in opposition to God, rebelling against God."[2] The world neither recognized nor responded to Christ. It is marked by unbelief, and is, therefore, something from which God's people ought to maintain a certain distance. They must certainly not love the world (1 John 2:15-17; James 4:4).

John's Gospel is rich in material on this point also. He presents this phase of kosmos in a series of antitheses or contrasts, for instance, light and darkness, spirit and flesh, above and below, et cetera. ("You belong to this world below, I to the world above. Your home is in this world, mine is not" [John 8:23]; "God is the source of my being. . . . Your father is the devil" [verses 42-44]; "I am the light of the world. No follower of mine shall wander in the dark; he shall have the light of life" [verse 12; cf. John 1:5; 11:9; 12:35, 46]).

"This world," in the sense of the forces that stand in opposition to the purposes of God, is parallel to the expression "this age," or the "present age" as we find it used in Paul's writings and in the Synoptics, for example, "this present age of wickedness" (Gal. 1:4; cf. 1 Cor. 1:20; 2:6-8; 3:19; Matt. 12:32; Mark 10:30; Eph. 2:2ff.). On the one hand, this world is contrasted with the world or "age to come," and on the other, with a world that is already here but is of a different kind, namely, "from above" (John 8:23; 18:36).

This third idea underlying the concept "the world"—creation that has turned away from its Creator and has become subject to "the power of the evil one" (1 John 5:19; cf. John 12:31; 14:30; 16:11)—is in the New Testament the most dominant of the three.

Human beings, whom God loved so much (John 3:16), are an intrinsic part of an order or system that has gone astray and that not only finds itself in opposition to God (Rom. 8:7) but feels that the alternative order or purpose of God is folly (1 Cor. 2:14). God's intention is to break through to those creatures made in His image, to open communication where communication has been virtually nonexistent, and to make humans see that it is the orders, systems, purposes, and goals other than His that are folly. He spares no cost to achieve this. Indeed, He sent to us His only Son.

But the world hated Jesus because of His determination to expose the folly of this world (John 7:7) and discredit its ruler (John 12:31). The contrast between the two worlds is sharp, and the hatred that "this world" felt for the Saviour was, after His departure, transferred to His followers (John 15:18; 17:14). Christ's followers have no choice but to continue to live in the world in that they share space with other people and work with the same organizations and systems (John 13:1; 17:11, 15) as those "of the world." Nonetheless, they are not of the world. "They no longer share the same character as the world because they belong to Jesus Christ, having received his word (John 17:14)."[3] As was Christ, so they are "strangers in the world" (verse 16). They belong elsewhere and will form a fellowship around Jesus Christ that expresses this.

Nevertheless, as the world was the scene of Christ's saving mission, in which He was motivated by love, so His similarly motivated followers are to continue His mission (verse 18). In this sense, then, lack of interest in the world is a missionary failure. Withdrawal from the world, be it for fear of contamination or for various monastic ambitions, has always been a poor solution for a people professedly concerned with mission.

It should be clear from what we have observed that, although the citizens of the world have gone astray and are without hope and without God and are strangers to the community of God's people (Eph. 2:12), God still has a tremendous interest in and openness to the world *as people.* This profound interest of God in people, which the followers of Christ are also to have and express, does not overlook the attitudes of the world in its gone-astrayness. For it neither recognized Christ ("The world, though it owed its being to him, did not recognize him" [John 1:10]) nor the Father ("O righteous Father, although the world does not know thee, I know thee" [John 17:25]) *nor the Holy Spirit* (Christ, speaking to His followers of the Comforter, says: "The world cannot receive him, because the world neither sees nor knows him; but you know him, because he dwells with you and is in you" [John 14:17]).

Therefore, it should not appear shocking or arrogant that we have in this study confessed a close affinity between Christ, the Spirit, and *the church* virtually to the exclusion of the world. Among His people Christ and the Spirit are not strangers. Outside—in the world—they are. The difference is one of faith and commitment. But while the Spirit is not in the world in the way that He is the gift to the believers and resident among them, He has a definite interest in the world, as did Christ. He desires to bring salvation to all while the light of day is still available.

The Spirit communicates salvation to the world by convicting it that "the Prince of this world stands condemned" (John 16:8-11). It is the death and resurrection of Christ and His subsequent ministry that exposes, discredits, and finally condemns the "Prince of this world." The Spirit does not do His work by presenting a physical appearance of Himself as did Jesus to the people of Palestine. The Spirit uses other physical agents—people and written words.

It is probably in this context that we shall have to understand Jesus' parting words to His followers as recorded in John 16:8-11. He said that He Himself must leave, and that when He had left He would send the Spirit, who would, through the disciples, convict the world of sin, of righteousness, and of judgment.[4]

Only the recognition that Christ was right, that He was in fact the one whom He claimed to be—which in Paul's thinking was proved by His resurrection and exaltation—will in the end discredit and disarm the ruler of this world. For that reason the Spirit's ministry is to present Christ with such conviction that people of the world are led to confess His lordship (John 15:26; 1 Cor. 12:3).

Believers were to be given power from on high (Luke 24:47-49) in the gift of the Holy Spirit (Acts 1:8), which would make them witnesses to the world. The Holy Spirit acts on the few *in the interest of the many.* This is seen in the bestowal of certain gifts on some of the members of the church in the interest of the whole church—a point we have made several times in this study. The same is seen in His coming with power to the believers as a whole in the interest of the whole world.

This means that to become a Christian is to become part of a community that is both *called* and *sent*—never just one of them. This is what one writer calls "the inward pull" and "the outward thrust,"[5] which are the dynamics of Christian living. On the one hand is the magnetism from Christ that draws believers together into a community, and, on the other, that propulsion from Christ which causes the same community to move outward into the open world as witnesses.

Consequently, to accept Jesus Christ and to receive the gift of the Spirit has importance not just for me and my immediate community (the church), but for the whole, unlimited, gone-astray world at whichever point I may make contact with it. Our baptism identifies us with a missionary body. Such is God's interest in the world.

We have observed that the Spirit's ministry to the world was conducted through agents—people, written words, etc. I can already hear the objection quite clearly: "Are you seriously saying that the Spirit can witness of Jesus Christ only through people and the Bible? I mean, are you trying to tell us that where Christian missionaries are not at work and where the Written Word is not available, the Holy Spirit has absolutely no other means of breaking through and making contact with human beings?"

No! Making categorical statements such as that would fail to recognize both the Spirit's resourcefulness and His untiring efforts to penetrate the darkness that envelops our gone-astray world. We have been told that "among the heathen are those who worship God ignorantly, those to whom the light is never brought by human instrumentality, yet they will not perish. . . . Their works are evidence that the Holy Spirit has touched their hearts, and they are recognized as the children of God."[6] Furthermore, "wherever there is an impulse of love and sympathy, wherever the heart reaches out to bless and uplift others, there is revealed the working of God's Holy Spirit."[7]

To confess to the almightiness of God is one thing. One does not doubt that humanly speaking, against all odds, the Spirit is immensely resourceful in breaking through darkness to touch a mind that is disenchanted with "the present world." Such an individual takes a posture of reaching upward and outward, searching, and laying bare responsive chords that are exceptionally sensitive. No one dare suggest any limits to the methods the Spirit may use to make contact with such a person.

It is, however, an entirely different thing to say that since a particular method has been used, is being used, and no doubt will be used, it is, therefore, the common, ordinary, and normal pattern anytime and anywhere. That is, unless one is also prepared to say either that there are a great number of equally effective ways for God to offer His solution in Jesus Christ to a fallen world and that the church with its human witnesses and Written Word are just two of these, or, as many mission theologians today will argue,[8] that "God's Spirit has always been at work in the cultures and faiths of men."[9] Christ, they say, is there in hidden form. He need merely be recognized or rediscovered without the frills of Western Christian traditions.

One suspects that this line of thinking is fostered by either an openness to the values of other cultures, a concerned effort to combat "Christian arrogance," or just sympathy—or a combination of them. It is difficult to see how the biblical picture of "the present world," how its message of Jesus Christ and the things He stood for (which people are asked to understand and relate to), how the message of salvation *only* in Christ can give any support to this idea of a diffused Christ and Holy Spirit within primal and non-Christian world religions. If their claim were true, why does not the New Testament make the same point? Instead, the message that comes through with great clarity is that the gift of the Spirit is inseparably tied to a personal encounter with the risen Lord.

What we finally arrive at is not the equality of opportunities for salvation inside the various world religions, but the missionary responsibility entrusted to the church. Her life is one of proexistence. Her calling and her gifts are for all. To be a Christian is ipso facto to be a missionary. To this end the Spirit is powerfully present and active. His interest never falters, although the church's uninterest or diverted interest will often fail Him.

"You will receive power when the Holy Spirit comes upon you; and you will bear witness for me in Jerusalem, and all over Judaea and Samaria, and away to the ends of the earth" (Acts 1:8).

---

[1] C. K. Barrett, *The Gospel According to St. John* (London: SPCK, 1972), p. 135.

[2] A. Richardson, *An Introduction to the Theology of the New Testament* (London: SCM Press, 1958), p. 207.

[3] G. E. Ladd, *A Theology of the New Testament* (Grand Rapids: Wm. B. Eerdmans Pub. Co.), p. 226.

[4] W. H. Griffith Thomas, *The Holy Spirit of God,* pp. 186, 187.

[5] D. Webster, *Unchanging Mission* (London: Hodder & Stoughton, 1965), pp. 64ff.

[6] Ellen G. White, *The Desire of Ages,* p. 638.

[7] ———, *Christ's Object Lessons,* p. 385.

[8] One of the more recent appearances of this thinking is that expressed by the "Christian Presence" series, edited by M.A.C. Warren, in which appeared works by K. Cragg (*Sandals at the Mosque* [London: Oxford University Press, 1959]) and John V. Taylor (*The Primal Vision* [London: S.C.M., 1963]).

[9] E. C. Webster, *Not Ashamed* (London: Hodder & Stoughton, 1970), p. 72.

Appendix

Why are so many people attracted to charismatic renewal movements? Or, to repeat the question asked earlier in our study, What does the existence of these movements tell the churches of today? The very fact that these movements exist, flourish, and have a remarkable magnetic attraction for many has a message the churches need to get.

Although charismatic movements—apart from historic Pentecostalism—may have lost some of their impetus, at least in some parts of the world, their basic appeal is not likely to die out. This appeal comes in waves and is, in a way, almost akin to existentialism. It is related to a profound despair and disenchantment with the status quo, both in one's personal life and in the life of the community. We will list some of the areas in which the appeal is quite noticeable.

1. Simon Tugwell, a Roman Catholic who has made an interesting examination of the subject, wrote: "Ours is an age of great spiritual revival; mysticism in all its forms is 'in.' And it is interesting to notice how united its voice is, from Zen Buddhism to Pentecostalism. . . . Hindus and LSD-trippers and Pentecostals all speak of extrasensory adventures and exploits with the same seriousness. Spiritualists, magicians, and Pentecostals all revel in spiritual healing, often with the aid of what they all call 'creative imagination.'"[1]

Here is a person who has tried to travel the road to a spiritually rich life by the way of liturgy and confessional creeds, to effective witnessing by way of evangelistic campaigns or other types of programmatic Christianity, and to personal victory through a mixture of prayer, faith, and self-discipline. But he still has the feeling that he has not quite made it. He feels that a spiritual "crossing of the t's and dotting of the i's" still remains. The idea grows upon him that a psychic experience is the ideal way to complete and enrich a spiritual life in need of just a little extra. Hence, the appeal is to something that is yet unexplored and that makes subtle claims.

2. The charismatic renewalist promises, "Come with us and 'your life will begin to have real power!' "[2] There is obviously an appeal in this—and what a promise to come after a period of spiritual depression! There are few things Christians want more than real power—power to cope with personal problems and to overcome timidity and be able to witness effectively. Then, of course, the implied promise of snap victories, instead of the long and laborious struggle of Christian growth, is not without appeal.

3. The renewalist goes on without a pause: "If you want to understand the New Testament you need the same experience that all its writers had."[3] What Christians do not want to understand the New Testament? Again, in a subtle fashion, it seems like an innocent call to a return to primitive Christianity. The call to such a return is being sounded by a vast number of Christians as the answer to apathy and apostasy in our churches. So if that is what the charismatic revivalist is leading us to, maybe it isn't too bad, we think. And slowly, albeit reluctantly, some parts of our defense mechanism are being demolished.

4. The renewal movements are at pains to stress that what they offer is not a new teaching. We are not asked to change the theological content of our faith. Rather, "a life

in the Spirit which belongs to the very nature of the church"[4] is offered. Persons are encouraged to seek new spiritual richness without having to compromise loyalty to their church or confession. Consequently, no one who becomes involved in charismatic movements need feel like a spiritual traitor.

5. The ecumenical emphasis is such as to attract many. It is being underlined that the charismatic movement is ecumenical, a bridge over the gulfs between the churches. It represents our common experience, we are told, whereas in our traditional churches we have been more conscious of the differences that separate us. Hence the emphasis is, "By our love they shall know that we are one."

6. The charismatic movement does not impose any intellectual burden on its followers. That is a welcome relief to many who have become weary of "cerebral Christianity." In the charismatic movement an intellectually reclined position ("my intellect lies fallow" [1 Cor. 14:14]) is preferred, especially for those who seek the experience of speaking in tongues.

7. Charismatic meetings are basically unstructured and nonliturgical. There is plenty of room for the spontaneous participation of individuals. "When you feel the Spirit come, you respond as He leads you!" This appeals to many people who have become disenchanted with their own liturgically structured churches that, in effect, reduce the congregation to a group of noninvolved recipients.

This list is by no means exhaustive. The appeals are as numerous as the needs of people are different.

A number of traps are built into these points of appeal. The most hazardous may well be in its anticerebral approach. If people believe that their intellect, mind, or understanding is not to be engaged in, they open themselves wide open to self-deception. How is one possibly to "test the spirits" with a mind that "lies fallow"? Even the most fundamental appeal to the authority of the Bible demands intellectual work.

The basic argument, which is false, is that because living the life of a Christian is for most people difficult, not without pain, and certainly a life of self-denial, something must be wrong with it. Christ never taught that discipleship would be without pains and great difficulties. Rather, the picture of a disciple is of one who carries a cross. The way of Christ contains no shortcuts. There is no such thing as a snap victory. The way is a long grind, with pains and defeats, but full of hope, promise, and assurance. The Bible knows of no alternative. Faith cannot be propped up artificially by an emotional session of "letting yourself go."

Of course we want to return to New Testament Christianity. That is what we are constantly seeking. But we cannot unwind history and in imagination place ourselves at a time in history where we are not. God meets the needs of His people *where they are,* but not always in the same fashion.

The suggestion found under point 4, that it is possible to cultivate an experience of religion without reference to teaching or dogma, is too ludicrous to be taken seriously. Experience and teaching shape each other and grow out of each other. We cannot embark on a new kind of religious experience and think that the content of our previous faith is unaffected by it all. That kind of a division does not exist.

As for the ecumenical emphasis, we can become so blind while looking on commonness that we become insensitive to both apostasy and syncretism. Again, the content of our faith and the critical and disciplined usage of our understanding are important. Why is conformity (or uniformity) of itself more Christian than the courage to be different?

In my view, the positive message coming from such renewal movements that should be given serious notice is that there is a profound need for many people (a) to find a greater warmth in Christian fellowship—to discover the experience that is to accompany teachings; (b) to become more involved in church services, to take part in the worship, and to respond—sharing faith and experience rather than merely sitting in the pew and receiving; and (c) to experience, hopefully as a result of the above, the nearness of God so that the prayer of the congregation may not be only for God to be present with them, but one of praise and thanks for the fact that He is present.

---

[1] Simon Tugwell, *Did You Receive the Spirit?* (New York: Paulist Press, 1973), p. 101.

[2] Dennis and Rita Bennett, *The Holy Spirit and You,* p. 75.

[3] *Ibid.,* p. 65.

[4] *Theological and Pastoral Orientations on the Catholic Charismatic Renewal,* a statement prepared by a group of Roman Catholic theologians at Malines, Belgium, May 21-26, 1974 (Notre Dame, Ind.: Word of Life, 1974), p. 37.